ROYAL RESILIENCE

OUR STORY OF SURVIVING AND THRIVING AFTER HURRICANE HARVEY

KENDRA KINNISON

To each of you that choose to enter the arena everyday.

"It is not the critic who counts; not the man who points out how the strong man stumbles, or where the doer of deeds could have done them better. The credit belongs to the man who is actually in the arena, whose face is marred by dust and sweat and blood; who strives valiantly; who errs, who comes short again and again, because there is no effort without error and shortcoming; but who does actually strive to do the deeds; who knows great enthusiasms, the great devotions; who spends himself in a worthy cause; who at the best knows in the end the triumph of high achievement, and who at the worst, if he fails, at least fails while daring greatly, so that his place shall never be with those cold and timid souls who neither know victory nor defeat."

THEODORE ROOSEVELT

CONTENTS

PREFACE

On August 25, 2017, Hurricane Harvey made landfall on the Texas Gulf Coast near Mustang Island. Our resort was significantly impacted, and this book shares our journey through the storm and first year of recovery.

We've decided to share our experiences in a documentary style, using messages and communications that were mostly captured in the moment. As the author of most updates to our Board of Directors and community, I'm narrating the backbone of the story.

However, there are dozens of voices and perspectives needed to bring our experiences to life and share them in a meaningful way. Throughout each chapter, you'll see contributions from our leaders, team members, and other partners. We've tried to clearly indicate those sections, and we've added an index where you can read more about each person in our story.

Before the storm, I would have described us as a close-knit and resilient team. Our location and the hospitality business often demand it. I could never have imagined how much stronger our bonds could be, and just how much we could endure together. I'm not sure if this is an experience I'd ever want to repeat, but I'm also very thankful to have lived it with this special group of people.

I hope this book is a testament to resilience, teamwork, faith, courage, and a spirit of service. I hope it inspires you to lock arms with your team and accomplish something special together. And I hope you'll write a book about that too.

We are #portroyalstrong, and this is our story.

Kendra K.

Kendra Kinnison
    General Manager, Port Royal Ocean Resort
    July 31, 2018

CHAPTER 1

LANDFALL

Wednesday, August 23

<u>1:45 PM</u>

I hit send.

Board Members -

I have spoken with the city, county, Daniel Carlisle, and Terri Adams with Schlitterbahn.

All recommendations are that we cease guest operations during the storm, given that Hwy 361 is likely to flood and power is likely to be disrupted. That means that emergency services may not be available, and guest phones would not be operational after a few hours. Terri, in particular, warned me of operating under that scenario after her experience in South Padre.

I would like to wait for the next weather update at 4pm today, but absent any major changes, this is how I think we should proceed.

My recommendation is that we close to guests tomorrow at 11am, and notify guests scheduled to arrive today of that plan and allow them to cancel.

If you strongly object to that scenario, I would like to know your thoughts.

Thank you,
kk

The decision was not an obvious one. At this time, the storm was not projected to be very strong – perhaps a category one or two at most. We'd been following it since Monday, praying that it turned or fizzled. For the last forty years, all storms eventually had.

But we're on a barrier island. It's not unusual to lose power several times a year for a few hours each, and that became uncomfortable quickly. In this case, we'd be taking care of over two thousand people for several days with no power, fragile communications, and limited emergency services – all in the blistering Texas heat.

We just couldn't take the risk, and we'd be putting our employees in an unfair situation as well.

.   .   .

I called my Board President, Jerry Ellis, continuing our conversation from earlier in the week. "You know what? I think we've got to evacuate," I said. He replied, "Well, it's your call. Do what we need to do. We've planned for this. Let's do it."

Emails from Board members confirmed our decision.

Agree.

Sounds wise. The TXDOT signs on the interstate are warning people not to drive to the coast.

Yes, plan for the worst. Always be safe, hope for the best.

2:00pm

We officially initiated our Emergency Action Plan.

Our Executive Team gathered with our Safety Manager, Bonney Maurer, to walk through our plans and checklists for each department. I don't think any of us have ever been more thankful for those big red binders with supply listings, checklists, and action items.

3:00pm

The timing was helpful. All our team members were gathered in the ballroom for our weekly all-hands meeting. Normally, we'd celebrate birthdays, reward shout-outs from guests on comment cards, and share background on any special events or groups.

Today was different. The air was thick with tension.

We announced that we would be ceasing operations and evacuating guests and owners. There was a gasp, and then waves of relief as we talked through key concerns.

We asked everyone to stay for their shifts tonight and to come in early tomorrow for a half day. We processed payroll a day early, ensuring that direct deposits and checks would be available Thursday, and we setup an employee hotline with RingCentral so that we could provide updates, even if our phone system was down.

We also asked the team to stay off social media and allow us to communicate to guests in an organized way.

3:30pm

We made our decision public and began contacting guests.

. . .

Our Facebook update read:

Due to the re-entry and strengthening of Tropical Storm Harvey in the Gulf of Mexico, we will effectively be closing the resort at 11am tomorrow, August 24. We plan to resume operations on Sunday, August 27th.

While we don't anticipate the storm to be severe, we do feel that this is our best option to keep both guests and teams safe.

All guests due to check-in tonight (8/23/17) are welcome to come stay, but will be required to checkout by 11am tomorrow (8/24/17).

Guests set to arrive Thursday, Friday and Saturday will be contacted by our reservations team to discuss options for rescheduling your stay and cancellations.

Of the dozens of comments, most were supportive. Some were frustrated that we were impacting their summer vacations.

Being in the hospitality business, it has always been our goal to ensure our guests have an enjoyable vacation; it's why we've developed our mission and vision - "To Create Memories to Last a Lifetime." Our teams take this mission in our guests' vacations personally, and letting our guests know that their vacations would be cut short or cancelled was certainly one of the hardest tasks our teams had to endure. However with safety in question, there was no other choice in our action.

STEPHAN NOACK, DIRECTOR OF REVENUE
AND MARKETING

7:47pm

Our pace was intense, but smooth.

Many families still checked in that evening. In most cases, they had begun their travels before our decision was communicated. It was a beautiful evening, and I couldn't help but savor the view at the pool.

We shared another update to our Board and core team:

We are contacting all guests and will not be open as a hotel after checkout tomorrow. So far, the feedback and commentary on social media is mostly positive.

We are also contacting the permanent residents to let them know our plans. Bonney is speaking with them to encourage staying elsewhere, particularly those with medical concerns.

Eight of us will be staying on property for the duration of the event, and we have planned accordingly.

We will be taking all possible unit precautions, placing patio furniture inside, and placing towels underneath patio and front doors, and using as many sandbags as we can. The winds do not appear to be the main threat - just lots of water.

I'm working on an update tonight for the owner portal. If you have other topic suggestions, be sure to let me know and we'll add to it.

Thank you all,
kk

I headed home, not knowing what tomorrow would hold, except that it would be very different from today.

Thursday, August 24

6:00am

I switched on the news for an update, packed my overnight bag, marked my list for items I still needed, and took a quick video of my home. I knew I was going all-in to work mode, and it might be a while before I was home again.

Driving into work that morning was different. I had packed a few important items and tried to anticipate how employees would respond to this unknown situation. I will never forget the view from our restaurant looking at the busyness at the pool. Our teams were working with intention. It was a little after 6 am, and everyone was focused on their job to complete. Emotions were certainly charged and thankful that a decision had been made to take care of property and then be with their families to weather the storm.

PAT BELL, DIRECTOR OF HR

9:30am

We held our daily Stand Up meeting, and talked through each element of our plan.

Our teams had already made tremendous strides in completing our preparations.

All furniture from our pool area was being brought inside or sunk in the pool. Housekeeping and other teams were moving patio furniture inside of each unit, and ensuring doors and windows were closed and secure. Office areas were being prepared and secured.

Mid-day

I received word that the Tropical Storm had been upgraded to a hurricane. I was just getting back into Corpus Christi for the last few items on the supply list and a lunch meeting that had been planned for weeks. I hustled through CVS and postponed the lunch.

Then I called Bonney.

Kendra: Bonney, let's walk through this one more time. I want you to double-check our logic and plan.

Bonney: Okay. The EAP has been completed, and we've confirmed our secure location.

Kendra: Are we sure this is within the boundaries of our plan to stay? Let's be sure we're not setting up anyone to put their life in danger.

Bonney: There's always risk, but we've limited it as much as possible. We have every supply on our list. We're surrounded by concrete, and we're 20 feet above ground.

Kendra: Are you completely comfortable with staying?

Bonney: I am.

Kendra: Okay, I am too. Let's button up and get ready.

Bonney: Sounds good. I'm picking up a few more supplies, and I'll be back there within the hour.

I rushed back to property. I was concerned that a checkpoint would be setup if a mandatory evacuation were declared.

And then there were five.

Everyone wanted to help. Several leaders wanted to stay on property to ride out the storm and yet, one by one, their family obligations required them to leave. We each understood and we looked around the table to see who was staying by choice. There was no idea how critical each person's role would be to execute this unknown adventure.

PAT

3:59pm

We sent this update to the Board -

Emergency Preparation

All of our Emergency SOP's have been executed by each department. We asked our teams to work until noon today, and they responded beautifully.

All of our buildings and units have been secured. Cabana furniture, carts, etc have been moved to the Ballroom. Pool furniture has been sunk in the middle pool. Patio furniture has been placed inside each unit, and towels have been used under doors where water is anticipated. Elevators have been brought to ground level and powered down. All buildings and doors have been locked or zip-tied.

Later this evening, we will use vehicles to block our entrance/exit at the welcome station.

We are in the process of making sand bags and will place them at vulnerable locations for as long as we are able.

We partially drained the ponds yesterday in preparation for reducing the pool levels as the rains come. This should help prevent flooding in the main building. Bonney will monitor and adjust.

If/when it is necessary to terminate gas lines or other utilities, we have identified the locations and will take those actions.

We intend to walk each unit daily to confirm that AC's are operational (as long as we have power) and to inspect for damage.

IT/Communications

All servers and computers have been powered down, and backups have been confirmed. Employees have been directed to call the Update Line on Saturday for further instruction - 361-400-2598. The owner dedicated line and ownerteam@ email have been updated. We are not staffing the front desk or answering the switchboard.

All reserved guests have been proactively contacted to notify of our closure. Reservations/Guest calls are being answered by RezForce, and they also have the script from the owner line. Social media is being answered and updated regularly.

We expect to lose internet and phones as the outer bands of the storm arrives tomorrow. We have radios that will work point-to-point, and we expect to be able to send text messages. We have plenty of Mophie portable chargers.

Occupancy

All guests have been evacuated. All owners have agreed to leave. Only one is still on property and has indicated she will leave today. All employees have been dismissed, except for the voluntary core team.

We are in the following units:

6205
　Brent Grant
　Matt Trent

6207
　Bonney Maurer
　Pat Bell
　Kendra Kinnison

Contact and emergency information is attached.

Safety

We are comfortable with our preparations. We have plenty

of food and water. We have flashlights, batteries, and basic tools, etc. We have generators and portable AC's for two units. We have first aid kits and plenty of supplies.

Bonney and I visited with the Captain at the Fire Station on Hwy 361, and we will provide them with our rooming list and contact information.

I am suspending the portion of the employee manual that prevents employees from having firearms on property. Bonney, Brent, and Matt have personal firearms with them, including a rifle. As the water comes over the dunes, we expect coyotes. We do not take this responsibility lightly, but felt it was prudent to be prepared to protect ourselves.

Please let me know if there is any portion of this update that you would like for me to post on the owner portal. Perhaps the top section?

I will continue to provide updates as we are able, and as there is relevant news. Please let me know if you have other questions.

I hope you all stay safe as well. It appears this could affect most of us.

kk

We gathered together for a family style dinner, and then went to bed early and in good spirits. The weather reports were indicating that landfall was expected mid-morning as a category two storm.

Friday, August 25

<u>6:16am</u>

Another update –

Since the last update yesterday, we have:

- Turned off both main gas lines supplying property.

- Walked each unit between 3-6am this morning to ensure property is fully vacated, front and patio doors are secured, patio furniture is indoors (except for very large tables unable to be moved), and air conditioners are operational.

- Fully secured administrative and other offices in preparation to shelter in place until the storm passes.

At this time, we are preparing 6207 (primarily) and 6205 to shelter in place for as long as necessary. Bonney has the lead in ensuring we have all appropriate supplies and have taken all precautionary measures. She is very well prepared for these scenarios, and we have reviewed these plans together many times.

We have internet access remaining, but not cell, and text is limited. Facebook is actually the most functional option. Most of my personal posts are public if you want to look there.

We feel confident in the concrete structure for winds,
could withstand flooding of 15ft, and are prepared if we
need to last several days without utilities or outside access.

Everyone is here voluntarily, and is free to leave at any
time. I have not asked anyone to stay reluctantly. Bonney
and I have discussed this many times, and we both prefer
our location to other possible options.

kk

2:23pm

By now, it was clear that the storm had intensified as it churned
in the Gulf.

Quick update - we are expecting to lose power soon.

We are sheltered in 6207 - myself, Bonney, Pat, Brent, and
Matt. Some pictures are attached. This unit is additionally
protected by the elevator shaft. We are also ready to
quickly divert to another unit in the event of damage.

It's going to be intense, but we feel good about our
preparations and prayers.

We are likely to have trouble getting messages out once we
lose power. Please do not panic.

We are getting creative with what is working to find an alternative way to communicate. We think we can get messages to Mellissa Shackelford and Martha Castro, both evacuated. They should be able to keep you updated, and post basic messages to our Facebook page so that others know that we have checked in.

We'll check in as soon as we can.

kk

The on-site team utilized mattresses from roll away beds and wood planks to secure the windows and doors.

With a high powered antenna, the team was able to
watch local news reports. They also had a full kit of
supplies and a generator.

As the storm was imminent, the text messages from friends and
family kept mentioning that the storm was picking up and was
going to be a category 3 or 4. There were offers to shelter us and
requests that we leave the property. I know it was nerve-
wracking for those who cared for us, but the decision was made
and leaving was just not an option.

We checked on each other's thoughts often, "Are you doing
okay?" we would ask. I remember a couple of honest
conversations about truly being concerned about being in
harm's way. Allowing us to talk freely was important. We were
as prepared as we could be ... and now we just had to wait.

Walking down the hallway was very eerie. It was very quiet,
and you could not even tell the storm was roaring around us. It
was getting later and we wanted to see what we could. A few of
us walked towards the end of hall and you could hear the fury
in the wind and the waves of the ocean. The rain had started

and we knew it was just a matter of time. Lots of deep sighs and hard swallows trying to calm our thoughts. Knowing we were going to be bunkered in "Fort Royal" gave us comfort. Waiting was the hardest part... we had to stay busy to keep from overthinking it.

Those of us who could, called our families to assure them that we were fine, prepared and in a concrete building high off the ground. Our team members checked on us every 15 minutes to give us updates. I remember Kendra's mother calling and for a fleeting moment, we could feel her hug through the phone. She was proud of us and wanted us to take care of each other.

PAT

4:24pm

Our last communication before landfall.

We just lost power. We'll keep you posted. So far, 6207 is holding up well.

CHAPTER 2

SUNRISE

BEFORE WE KNEW IT, the storm was over. We survived, and each of us had a different perspective.

First thing I remember after the storm, it was super early. The wind was still blowing pretty hard so you could hear glass and debris moving around through the hallways. There was still some rain coming down.

As we woke up, we started walking outside and you could see all kinds of debris in the breezeways. A lot of broken glass. Pieces of the roof. We took our time going really slow and taking it all in.

We went down to the end of the building and looked out toward the bay. That was the first real image where it was apparent what had happened. You could see the seagrass, power lines, trees, water, and flooding on the ground.

The stairwells were full of debris. The whole time, the wind was still blowing pretty strong, so we weren't really sure if it was safe yet. I checked my phone to see if there was any signal yet - I wanted to get ahold of my family to make sure they knew I was alright. I had my dogs here, so I was trying to figure out how I could take them out. We made our way down the stairwells to the ground floor. We had to go very slow.

There were pieces of the roof, AC units, and natural debris everywhere. There was some kind of windblown grass and dirt mixture all over the buildings. It was like nothing I've ever seen before. It was like, you saw everything, but you weren't sure exactly what you were looking at. There was a big cone-looking thing in the parking lot, but it was actually a buoy that had made it all the way from the bay. That made us realize how bad the storm surge must have been.

I had my truck in the parking garage and assumed it had taken a lot of damage. I went to check it out. There was this yellow stuff all over it. It turned out, the wind had blown so hard that it pulled the paint off of the yellow speed bumps in the garage and against my truck. Other than that, there was no real damage.

I was pretty relieved that my truck was alright. We had the Gator downstairs because before the storm we had been getting supplies. We all went out on the Gator to drive around and then ended up going on foot. We walked toward the lobby and saw the ACs that had come off the roof, and realized that wasn't a safe place to be.

We went around to the front through the lobby doors and realized the damage was pretty significant. There was standing water, ceiling tiles down, and it smelled very wet.

We quickly realized that that area had taken the majority of the damage because the stairwell was almost completely blocked with pieces of roof, palm fronds, and debris.

MATT TRENT, FOOD & BEVERAGE
MANAGER

We decided to raid the kitchen, crawling through all kinds of debris to get up the stairs. We grabbed steak and shrimp, and Matt grabbed a huge bucket of Nutella.

BONNEY MAURER, SAFETY MANAGER

We went straight from waking up to walking around, then realized we needed to eat. We were all very tired - none of us got much sleep during the storm. We also had no power and no AC.

So we wanted to do something to lift everyone's spirits. We found some New York strip steaks in the restaurant, grabbed charcoal and lighter fluid in the Port Store, and started grilling. It was starting to rain so starting up the pit was a bit of a challenge.

At some point, you just have to laugh.

Realizing we just survived a Category 4 hurricane, we couldn't get mad about little stuff anymore. I got the pit going and grilled our steaks. I would cut up the steaks, then Kendra and Bonney would pass by in the Gator and take some.

BRENT GRANT, GUEST SERVICES
MANAGER

The on-site team woke up Saturday morning, thankful and ready to start the hard work of checking units and other concerns on property.

One of the first things I remember - Kendra and I were cruising around on the Gator, snacking on steak and trying to get a cell phone signal out to let everyone know we made it through.

Kendra said, "Let's try to go down to the boardwalk to see if we can get service there." I thought, "oh no. I don't think it will even

*be there still." But we got down there and I was amazed to see it
was still standing.*

*I remember it seemed so peaceful. There were birds out in
the water.*

BONNEY

---

*My first thought was, Damn. I've been here ten and a half years
and never have seen property in this state. It was such a shock.
This place is like a second home to me. I've never seen anything
like it.*

BRENT

---

*I just remember that I was looking at the damage and there was
a lot of clean up and work to do, but I didn't realize how much
until we started digging into it.*

*That debris, grass, and mud was literally caked onto
everything.*

*The Cabana Bar and Grill were a total loss. There was standing
water as high as the grills. Palm trees were snapped in half, so
the high winds were pretty evident. Instantly, I started thinking
about my home. Even though I had gotten my dogs and myself*

out of there, I was still concerned about my home and what happened in Port Aransas. It was such a weird feeling not knowing anything because there was no cell service and no news. It was very surreal to be so disconnected. Once we were able to get service by the boardwalk, I reached out to my family let them know I was ok. That was all the cell service I had that day.

MATT

Saturday, August 26th

9:36am

I shared this update to Facebook.

We are safe and uninjured. We have plenty of supplies. Connection is limited, but there's no need to worry.

For detailed updates, contact my Mom.

10:56am

I knew that the Board would want to know how the property fared, so I sent an update with the basics.

Good morning!

I'm glad we were able to keep getting messages out. Our Fort Royal held up just fine.

I would like to have a conference call today to discuss next steps and communications. Does 1pm work for y'all? If so, Noack please set us up with a call in number.

This is very preliminary, but my initial thoughts are that we will need to be fully closed for 2-3 months for critical repairs, and that it will likely take 6-9 months for a full restoration. I can share a more detailed damage report on the call.

It is likely the news will start showing pictures, so I want us to stay ahead of that if possible.

We have found a few spots with reliable connection. Oddly enough, I am typing from the Boardwalk. ;-)

kk

It was evident that we needed to regroup as soon as possible. I scribbled my thoughts on the only paper I could find. This would become the agenda for our next emergency board meeting.

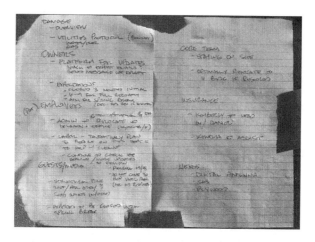

Kendra utilized paper scraps in order to make notes for the upcoming conference calls and discussions.

1:00pm

The Board approved the following measures:

1. Relocation of the administrative operations to the Corpus Christi building.
2. All utilities be turned off and only turned back on individually as each unit is assessed for safety.
3. Media and owner messaging be drafted and sent to the Board for approval tomorrow.
4. Core team is authorized to remain on property as long as needed.
5. Employees will be asked to return to work on September 5th with a few individuals returning sooner as needed.
6. Security concerns will be addressed with our vendor APS.
7. Kimberly Dusek will serve as insurance point person and will keep the board apprised along the way.

Jerry volunteered to answer emails from owners, directing them to the Owner Portal for the official statement forthcoming. We also realized that we may need to relocate the November Annual Meeting to a different location.

The meeting was adjourned at 2:02 pm.

I initially thought that it would take 6-9 months to recover.

I was trying to communicate that there was significant damage, but not catastrophic. I didn't have any understanding of the realities of the insurance process. I also didn't have any idea that we would be without power and water for a month, and how that would impact the timeline.

Before this, I thought the most damage you will have is the day after the storm. The reality is that the damage continues to get worse every single day, and you have to make efforts to stop it and stabilize before rebuilding.

8:15pm

_____

Owners,

As you know, Hurricane Harvey made landfall last evening very near Port Royal. We have been in contact with our on-site team for the duration of the event - from making the decision

Wednesday to cease operations Thursday, preparing the resort in advance of the weather, and now in the security and rebuilding efforts. The team is safe, secure, and in good spirits.

We will need more time and professional expertise to confirm our initial assessments as conditions are not yet safe enough for a full inspection. These are our preliminary indications:

Structurally, Port Royal appears to have fared well, particularly all concrete buildings. Building 2, the pool area, our food outlets, and about 15% of units in 3 and 6 buildings have been impacted. Buildings 4 and 5 appear to be mostly unharmed, except for one corner where flying debris caused damage.

Our goal is to have an initial damage assessment of each unit by Wednesday, August 30. We will share this information in the Owner Portal.

At this time, the resort does not have electricity, water, or gas service. The City has not provided a timeline on when this infrastructure will be repaired. The team has also disconnected each service, and will only restore them to each unit/building as it is safe to do so.

We have already contacted our insurance team and have begun the process of filing claims. In addition to our property policies, we also have a business interruption policy that begins coverage on the 7th day after interruption. It provides for replacement rental income to owners and covers expenses such as employees. We will provide more details as they are available.

If you plan to come to Port Royal personally to assess your unit or for contents claims, please be patient and follow all safety instructions from the team. It is strongly recommended that you wait until at least Monday as there are many downed power lines and other hazards on Hwy 361. Because of safety concerns, you will need to be escorted during your time here, and no one will be allowed to stay beyond 7pm.

We are in the process of relocating our administrative offices to our call center in Downtown Corpus Christi. Initial information indicates that building was not impacted by the storm. Our goal is to resume administrative operations on Tuesday, September 5th.

Please refrain from contacting employees directly as they have very limited connectivity, and are focused on securing the property to prevent further damage, provide documentation for insurance claims, and begin clean up and repairs as soon as possible.

Your Board is in communication with the team daily. We will provide updates in the portal every 3 to 5 days, and will email for significant messages. You may email us at Board@port-royal.com with specific questions, and we will respond as swiftly as possible.

While we would prefer not to deal with events like this, we are confident in our planning, preparation, and response. Together, we will restore Port Royal to its full potential.

Best regards,
    Jerry Ellis, President

For the rest of the day, we stuck around property and inspected as much as we could. Some people stopped by to check on us.

We couldn't get into Port Aransas so I knew I couldn't see my house. I was trying to figure out what I would do because I didn't have anywhere to go. We all ended up staying on property.

We worked on getting generators and situating rooms to try and make them more comfortable. Most of the day was pretty gloomy because the storm was still around. I was glad that we weren't hurt, but it was...I had no idea what the future was going to be. I didn't know if I was going to have a job or somewhere to live.

All in all, I was happy that we made it through ok.

MATT

There was no AC. We could barely sleep because of the heat.

I took the couch and slid it all the way to the balcony door, then opened the balcony door to sleep in the breeze. We didn't stay up too late that night because we were so exhausted.

We kept hearing different noises - the storm seemed to create a lot more bangs, bumps, and creaks. You could also hear the coyotes out looking for food. It was like a ghost town. It was so dark and eerie.

If you were outside and night looking around - to see this place so empty, with nothing going on...it was like walking into an old abandoned house.

BRENT

The quiet.

You never realize how much sound is around you until there's absolutely nothing because there's no power.

BONNEY

I had no idea how critical these first days would be to our overall recovery.

Sunday, August 27th

One board meeting was not enough. There were still several topics that needed to be addressed.

The board meeting began at 2pm and lasted for about 90 minutes. I shared a more detailed update and our plans for triage. I was focused on what our teams could do.

During the call, I was in favor of letting our teams be in charge of safety and remediation. Then right after we hung up, Kimberly Dusek called me back. In the kindest way possible, she shared that while she wasn't there, from what I had described, she thought I was underestimating what the process would entail with keeping people safe and getting stabilized.

More than likely, this would be more than we could handle internally. Gratefully, I thanked her for the correction and advice.

Then I called Daniel Carlisle. I told him, "I just had a call with Kimberly. She thinks it's not a good idea to do this on our own, that we probably need someone professional to step in. What are your thoughts?" He agreed. He also said that we have a duty under our insurance policy to aggressively mitigate any further damage.

I think it was then that he said, "I just met a company in the parking lot that was here because of a contract with H-E-B, but their damage isn't all that significant so they're getting ready to move on to Houston if no one here needs any help." We agreed it would be a good idea to meet with them.

9:00pm - Meeting with Signature Group

I was already in the area working on some assisted living facilities and a supermarket business. One of my sales guys was at a hotel that we had been working on. He had a big RV parked in the building where Daniel Carlisle was working. Daniel walked up and struck up a conversation with him. Just from that, we found out about Port Royal and drove out to meet with Kendra.

During our first meeting with Kendra at about 9pm that Sunday night, we struck up a conversation. I gave them our references and I laid out the way I saw the project going. We needed to remove moisture, get power, air circulation and dehumidifiers, then pinpoint all of the damage using thermal imaging and moisture mapping, and remove all damaged materials. To do that, we would first need to remove debris using heavy equipment to access everything, and to make sure all health and safety risks were removed or marked off.

My initial thought coming onto property was the damage to building 2. Of course that was the absolute worst damage because the roof was completely gone and the units were all destroyed. That was when I initially thought wow, you have a good amount of damage. We looked at buildings 3 and 6 and saw some missing roof and AC units hanging down. We toured a few units in those buildings. Every one of them had some form of water damage. I knew then that this was going to be a fairly large project. We needed power and air circulation fast, before really bad things happened to the buildings.

As we read the walls the moisture mapping showed a lot more water inside than people realized. I figured the project, with no hiccups, would be about 3 months just for restoration. I wasn't really focused on reconstruction at that time, because we needed to make sure everything was dry and all damaged materials were moved out before we worried about anything else.

I'm known for handling multiple very large projects and bouncing around, but I could tell the way this property was designed - multiple buildings, all forms of damage, all forms of contractors needed - it was going to be a very large project and consume a lot of time. I told Kendra, "If you choose to go with Signature Group, I will dedicate myself to Port Royal until it's complete," and to this date, I'm still here at least every week.

RIAN GLASSCOCK, SIGNATURE GROUP

CHAPTER 3

THE RALLY BEGINS

Monday, August 28th

3:36am

Restless and hot, I tried to focus on keeping things moving forward and communicating often. I sent another update to the Board.

After meeting with Daniel and talking with Kimberly, we met with a mitigation company called Signature Group last night.

Kimberly will be reviewing their contract, and we will be checking references first thing this morning. They are also doing work for HEB.

If all is confirmed, we will likely engage them today with two priorities - prevent mold and secure high-risk safety concerns. We are early and they still have labor capacity and equipment. For example, this could ensure generators and portable ac's in otherwise good units. They will provide exact protocols. I'm just giving an example.

After speaking with Daniel and understanding more about our coverages, I agree this is a critical step. I do not believe there is time or bandwidth for another call this morning. I will consult with Kimberly and Daniel before proceeding, and I will call Jerry for final Approval.

We are working to get admin going at the downtown office and are starting the videos this morning. That is the best next two steps we can take to restore detailed owner communications. It will likely be Tuesday before the fruits of these efforts show.

I very much appreciated Daniel's visit last evening. Having a friendly face and his coaching was invaluable. I believe he intends to come back by today to check in. I am touring the property with Signature Group about 10am.

For time-sensitive communication, text is best. We are finding more spots on property that have that much reception.I'm heading back upstairs and will get back out about 6am. We do have at least one full-time security guard 24/7 going forward.

I appreciate each of you.

kk

4:45am

We didn't expect to have electricity, but not having running water for so long was a surprise. While not our first choice, our hot tubs - no longer hot - sanitized with some chlorine helped us clean up a bit.

With that, we created a new rule: Boys weren't allowed to leave their rooms before sunrise. If only the snakes had been equally as cooperative.

I think this is when I truly understood that life was going to be different for a long time.

The on-site team frequently used hot tubs, at that time "cold dips," as a means to keep clean during the long hot days.

We were wiping ourselves with baby wipes for a "shower" - finding restrooms to use in building 6... and marking off which ones were used. We filled up toilet tanks with buckets to flush.

BRENT

(Laughing) We are some creative folks. Matt had the idea first - one of the main things about not having A/C and the summer humidity - getting clean is one of the biggest priorities. Matt had the idea to bathe in the hot tub. I got all the debris out of them, shocked them, and we started using them as bathtubs. The day we got port-o-potties - we were all so excited because we didn't have to figure out where we could go again.

BONNEY

7:01am

In my attempt to continue communication with everyone on the outside who was concerned, I posted another video update to Facebook.

It looks like I'm going to be even more acquainted with this 25 acres by the time this adventure is over. Our basic needs are covered, and the rebuilding process begins tomorrow. I know we will come back strong.

During the first few hours of Monday morning, I was checking references for Signature Group with Kimberly. By mid-day, we signed the contract, and the reinforcements started to roll in.

Signature Group brought in truckloads full of equipment - everything from dehumidifiers and blowers, to generators and a full power distribution system. The teams went to work stabilizing the property to where no further damage would occur.

I was humbled and grateful to have people that knew the next steps and what to expect.

We plan for these storms year round, and we have resources across the country that we work with. Everyone helps each other out, so we are usually able to mobilize pretty fast.

We brought in labor and supervisors to walk the property and get familiar with it. The first day or two we had about 30-40 people there. We peaked at about 100 workers in late September.

One thing people don't realize, there's not a lot of local help when storms like this happen. So we brought in people from all over the country. We had to facilitate housing and food for them. People work a lot better on a full belly.

We coordinated our own resources, including 18 wheelers and box trucks full of drying equipment, dehumidifiers, fans, mops, brooms, shovels, small and large tools to cut and remove drywall and damaged cabinets. We called a power company to get generators to run each building. We brought in our own distribution cords called spider boxes, which we needed to run power down the hallways and plug in our equipment.

There were a lot of things we brought in that you wouldn't normally think about like ice, fuel, and a makeshift shower setup so Kendra didn't have to bathe in the hot tub. We also brought in mobile command centers for us and Port Royal.

RIAN GLASSCOCK, SIGNATURE GROUP

Throughout our previous off-seasons, David Vinson was instrumental in our large construction projects, and had advised me as I took on the additional role of Interim Director of Facilities during the Summer.

I would often reach out to him for advice on technical matters and could certainly use his expertise during our journey. But he'd had surgery the week before the storm, and I was hesitant to reach out.

But like clockwork, on Monday morning - he was there, and we were thrilled to see him.

.   .   .

When he arrived, I immediately introduced him to Rian, and the two of them quickly became the core of our recovery.

David took a slightly more long term view with structural assessing. Rian focused on our urgent safety and water concerns, with more immediate manpower and equipment.

We learned quickly that water damage can be misleading and not as obvious as the visible wind damage. We walked many condos that seemed to be in good condition. It wasn't until Signature brought in their infrared cameras that we realized just how wet everything was.

I had closed on a house 3 days prior to the hurricane, and I had surgery the day after we closed on the house. When the hurricane hit, I told my wife, "I have to get down to Corpus Christi." I went out to property as soon as the roads were open. When I got there, to be honest, I thought 'oh crap'. I knew what the property was before, and I knew the expectations of owners and guests. I thought, 'we have a lot of work ahead of us.'

At that point, you forget about surgeries and houses and you just need to get to work. For me, it was a split second of taking it in. Then I switched my mindset to attacking the problems. Usually after a storm like that, everyone is in a rush to get contractors. Luckily we were able to get roofers, exterior walls, and Signature Group who brought in all immediately needed contractors. We started cleaning up and identified what needed to be done next.

I had no doubts about Rian and his team. He is very professional. You spend 5 minutes with him and you know what he is capable of, and he proves it. Kendra, Rian, and I quickly became what I refer to as "the group." We were the nucleus of the recovery process from the very beginning. It was a partnership. We would come up with a plan of action, execute, come back and debrief, then work through the issues. In the areas where we didn't have an idea of what to do, we tried to reach out to others who did have a better expertise. Sometimes, you just have to go with logic. That can be scary, but you just have to do it.

Amtech focuses on what is called the "building envelope" - the roof, walls, insulation, etc. We are an engineering and architectural firm so we specialize in designs and specifications for projects. We have the expertise and tools for assessment of problems. My role in the process was to come up with logical steps to move forward. That included mitigation, assessment, and getting contractors. Then there was the management piece - overseeing and evaluating the process, then circling back to reassess and tweak as you go. Signature Group specializes in water mitigation and construction. That's why our partnership makes sense and works so well - Amtech looks at the project from a design and engineering perspective and the project as a whole, then Rian and Signature Group are the strong arm. They come in, take the project plan, and make it happen.

DAVID VINSON, AMTECH SOLUTIONS

Kendra Kinnison meets with David Vinson from
AmTech Solutions, Rian Glasscock from Signature
Group and David Day of Casa Engineering.

Tuesday, August 29

While we were fairly quick to adapt to the primitive living environment, the challenges of mosquitos and the lack of utilities was setting in. Adding to the complexity was keeping owners safe as we escorted them to their condos.

I shared more in Facebook video updates:

It's pretty rough out here...and in fact this is already quite cleaned up. Our structural engineer told us today that he thinks a boat struck our 2 building - the lobby building - and started the chain reaction of damage through this area.

The team shovels seagrass that came from the bay during Hurricane Harvey to help clear our driveway.

As a result of the storm, air conditioners had become unsecured from the roof and were falling off of the building. Other hazards included falling pieces of roofing, missing railings, and flammable seagrass.

So this seagrass - I think as everybody knows - the storm came from the bay side, which is a little bit interesting. And so it carried all of the sea grass from the highway - Highway 361 - all the way up to our parking garages.

If you're familiar with Port Royal, you know that's a pretty good distance... and we've had backhoes today that were able to clear this for us so that we didn't have to do it by hand anymore. You can see the awesome pile of seagrass that has been piled up over here and gotten off our roads. I would say it is a good 8 feet tall in some places and this covered our entire driveways until today.

We cleared as much as we could by hand but getting that backhoe was just awesome. So we've cleared our roadways because this stuff is super flammable so if you've got any of it laying around I would definitely get it away from your house, I wouldn't smoke around it, I wouldn't start your cars around it. It is definitely not fun to have nearby.

8:15pm

I continued to update Facebook to let friends and family know our progress and conditions:

Thoughts from Day 6 so far ....

- Snakes are everywhere. Wear gloves to pick things up.
- All this seagrass is very flammable. Don't allow folks to smoke anywhere near it. (Don't ask me how I know.)
- If you want to be supportive but aren't sure how, go read the cliff notes from the book 'Option B.'

Wednesday, August 30

6:59pm

As the big equipment rolled in and the teams finished up for the day, I kept up my daily recaps on Facebook:

If you see the guys in the orange shirts - they are with a company called Signature Group, and they have just been awesome.

They have mobilized very very quickly, and we are excited about all they are going to do to keep Port Royal Strong for us. Of course, we've got all of our awesome team members as well but this group adds a supplement and a skill set and a set of resources that we are super excited to have.

We've got some awesome partners helping us - shout out to Signature Group has been fantastic, Amtech and Port Enterprises - two folks we have worked with in the past that were already out here today making plans. So we expect to get going pretty quickly.

Signature Group is very well versed in not only looking at the damage at the time, but how to minimize that damage. AmTech's specialty is construction management, so they focused on the future work.

David was very well spoken and a seasoned construction manager. So we started working together and bouncing ideas from two different spectrums of the construction industry. We meshed well together and managed to start building a portfolio with an overview of damage and what needed to happen to stop the damage from continuing to occur. Together, we compiled documentation, pictures, etc. to build our case for insurance.

RIAN

This was a key turning point for me, as I realized that it wasn't solely my responsibility to lead the physical repair of the property. Instead, I would be the communication hub and facilitator to keep us moving forward. I trusted Rian and David, and I knew that I could not have a better team working to make Port Royal Strong again.

My role would be to engage our key stakeholders and ensure each group was getting the information they needed at the time they needed it.

Sunday, September 3rd

This was a day that all of us were incredibly thankful for. Our "quality of life" trailer arrived and was set up. This included both an innovative shower system, as well as a washer and dryer.

A portable shower station and washer/dryer station
was setup in one of our parking lots.

Someone brought in a makeshift trailer. There was a shower, washer/dryer, big water tank, with a compressor to push water into the shower. It was running water. We didn't care if it was hot; just to have a shower was huge.

It was a trip. It was probably 4' x 4', so a tall guy like me trying to shower under a 5' shower head was pretty funny. I had to take linen sheets and curtain it around so no one could see. I probably mooned multiple people on 361. It was not easy. We had to get dressed and everything in that one spot.

BRENT

Saturday, September 9th

11:36am

With so many moving parts on property, I found it helpful to outline each step in emails to our Board.

Board members -

I'm using these updates to keep you informed of our efforts and provide status updates on key initiatives.

In general, I believe that we are getting in an operational rhythm and have planned weekly touchpoints with key advisors and partners.

We were also able to communicate to displaced employees that they have six weeks of paid leave to focus on their personal matters. They will be checking in with HR weekly, and we have provided counseling resources and a steady supply of gift cards. That list is approximately 20 people currently.

David Vinson, Rian Glasscock, and I met for several hours yesterday to map out our overall outline and determine our meeting and communication rhythms. I am very comfortable and confident in this team and approach. Everyone works well together and has the same standards of excellence.

We will each complete reports every Friday/Saturday, review them Sunday/Monday, meet together each Monday afternoon, and aim for an external communication each Tuesday. This would mean that we could reliably share an owner update each Wednesday.

I soon found comfort in a daily rhythm.

Mosquitos became a problem soon after the storm. Bonney and Kendra took on the duties of spraying the property to help control the swarms.

In case you're curious, this is what a 'normal' morning in disaster recovery looks like. Starting early is critical to stay ahead.

- 5:00-6:30am Quiet work (communications & plan day)
- 6:30-8:00am Morning Duty (generators, pest control, urgent items)

- 8:00-8:45am Exercise (usually swim)
- 8:45-9:00am Shower
- 9:00-10:00am Partner Meetings & Calls
- 10:00-10:30am Team Safety/Stand Up Meeting
- 10:30-11:00am Regroup with Owner Escort Team

CHAPTER 4

OUR FIRST TEAM MEETING

Sunday, August 27, 2017

WE SHARED an update to our employee hotline.

"Thank you all for calling the Port Royal Employee Hotline. Our on-site team is fine and we have sustained some property damage, but we're focused on clean up and our next steps. HR and administrative offices will be relocated to our call center in downtown Corpus Christi. All administrative staff are asked to report to the call center at 10am on Tuesday, August 29th. All full-time employees are asked to report to Port Royal property on Tuesday, September 5th at 10am. Part time and seasonal employees, please check with your manager for your individual status.

The roles needed during the next coming weeks will be physically demanding. Our traditional roles will be on hold while we clean up and organize property. Employee priorities should continue to be your home and family. All checks will be distributed from our HR office at the downtown call center.

Please continue to check the Port Royal Strong Facebook for property updates. We know there are lots of questions. We ask that you please be patient while we make decisions based on the information that we have on hand. There is lots of work to be done and we will do it all together. Take care and thank you."

Throughout the first week, we knew employees were itching to get back to property, take in what had happened, and help get us back up and running. We also knew it wouldn't be that simple.

Our employees were asked to stay updated by calling our dedicated employee hotline. At this time, we only had one mass communication system to relay updated information to all of our team members. Communication became Pat's number one focus.

Making the decision to bring our employees back on property was difficult. We wanted to ensure we could be there for our team members; their health, safety, as well as their emotional state. This was our main priority.

Our property had changed quite a bit, to say the least. We simply wanted to prepare everybody for what they were about to see. We quickly pivoted from simply assessing the property to thinking how our employees weathered the storm. We set up an emergency line for employees to call to receive updates.

Who would have ever guessed how critical that would become to keep our team connected.

At least one-third of our employees were affected some way by Hurricane Harvey. When we reached out to each team member, we asked two critical questions. Are you safe and, is your home okay?

It was at this time, Port Royal Strong was born. We had weathered the storm and, like the palm trees on property that did not break, neither did we. We are #PortRoyalStrong.

PAT

Tuesday, September 5th

<u>9:00am</u>

Today, we would reunite with our employees, and let them take in the property for the first time since the storm. We knew they would need some time to adjust to our new reality.

Many of the teams didn't realize the extent of the damage at first, as there was a lot of progress throughout the first week. But a quick walk around property seeing the piles of debris, the black pool, and 8 foot piles of seagrass was definitely eye opening.

.   .   .

Reality started to hit.

The teams gathered in what used to be our lobby area to hear our "new reality" and what our next steps would be.

We were crammed into the lobby area. Employees used coolers, luggage carts, and whatever furniture was left from before the storm. There was a heavy smell from the wet carpet, the ground was sticky from glue residue, and the sound of loud blower fans filled the room. Breakfast tacos donated by Stripes lined the tables.

How were we going to rebuild? Were we going to get paid? I knew it was going to be a long journey. I was sad.

What was before the storm was no longer there. It was really surreal, one day we were checking in 150+ people and then the next we didn't have a front desk.

CRYSTA STEWART, GUEST SERVICES
REPRESENTATIVE

As the meeting started, you could see the relief on their faces as we shared our next steps. Employees heard the much needed news: We still have jobs, we are still getting paid, and we are working on our plan for recovery.

Many of our own team members faced destruction in their personal lives, but still showed up to help rebuild a place they love.

Our team listened to a property update for those that had not been in contact with us. Safety manager, Bonney, briefed our team on the possible and visible safety precautions our team should follow to ensure the safety of everyone around.

Our employees, regardless of previous positions pre-Harvey, were assigned to groups based on their work ability and knowledge of certain tasks. We had teams cleaning seagrass from around property, assessing damages to rooms documenting the affected areas we could see with the bare eye. Our aquatics team members worked on removing large pieces of roof from building 2 that had blown off due to the wind.

Along with our team members were multiple of our individual condominium owners. These key volunteers helped assist our team escort other owners, insurance adjusters, and guests around property assuring safety protocols were executed.

PAT

Our Front Desk staff were recruited as property escorts in order to help owners access their units safely.

It felt like as if I was inviting people into my home. I had been here for six days however, it felt like we were here for a month. Having been here with a select few people for those few days, we got close real quick. The feeling of uncertainty, fear, and all having different emotions to the situation filled the air. Before everyone arrived on property, we had to get the property ready to have our employees back. Like I said, it was like inviting someone over to your home. There was some clean up that needed to be done as well as determining where our team was going to park. However, when our teams did begin to arrive, I felt a sense of relief. Seeing familiar faces was nice. It was comforting, just like seeing family you hadn't seen in a while. We shared stories, all while making sure everyone was safe and okay.

MATT

I didn't know the extent of damage that was done. We didn't know what exactly was going to happen. Where were we going to start? There was so much clean up to do. After walking through the pool area, I realized how much work had to be done. All the cabanas we had spent countless hours building were gone; metal screws were the only remembrance of those cabanas. I knew it was my job to get the pool back to normal.

JOHN GRANT, POOL TECHNICIAN

Looking back, that morning was when I realized we were a part of something special.

We all had a willing attitude. Due to my experience working here for over six years, I was open to whatever came my way. I

*felt the devastation after pulling into property seeing the mess
and how dirty the pool was. What used to be blue was now
pitch black. The passion I felt to clean our property gave me a
sense of relief. I then appreciated what we had before Harvey
and, I knew we had to get that back. We would get through this.
Working with other departments was such an eye opening
experience. Everyone was as willing as I was to accomplish our
daily tasks. It was rough, but somehow we pushed through. We
all fed off of each others energy to get through the days. I am
#PortRoyalStrong.*

RENEE TILLEY, HOUSEKEEPING
SUPERVISOR

Wednesday, September 8th

Things were moving fast, although it often felt like living in slow
motion. With so much more to do on property, we also had a
business to run.

---

*For the first time post-harvey, our Human Resources and
accounting teams were due for their bi-weekly responsibility of
running payroll. As many of you know, running payroll for
several hundred employees during a normal period of operations
is quite difficult. Due to the lack of power and resources on
property, we were forced to send our team to our reservations
center to ensure our team members were paid on time. After
receiving key information from HR, we grabbed necessary*

items needed to process payroll and headed to downtown Corpus Christi. Our accounting team ran payroll in circumstances we had never had to deal with before.

Sitting in a cubicle with nothing but a laptop and a portable wireless printer placed on the floor, our team was able to reach their deadline. All of our employees got paid.

JOHN REYES, CONTROLLER

Our reservations and front desk teams worked through our hotel operations system to reach out to our upcoming guests and cancel reservations for the next two months. While we didn't know just how long we would be closed, we knew we had to refund deposits and help our guests plan.

There was a process. First, we had to prepare my team. Next, we had to gather all info, create spreadsheets and divide the cancellations between team members.

Knowing the calls would be difficult, we had to prep our team with what to say and how to say. In the end, it was easier said than done. Staying professional and knowledgeable was most important; People didn't understand that we were destroyed by a hurricane. Most people we called heard about it, but didn't know the extent of the damage.

I felt bad for the team because they took the brunt of it.

MELISSA DIXON, RESERVATIONS MANAGER

Having to talk to guests was difficult, especially when it is someone on chemo with their last vacation and having to cancel those... you feel like you're to blame.

SARAH ZIEGLAR, RESERVATIONS
SUPERVISOR

Teams continued to sort through offices and box up any left over equipment, documents, and supplies and transport them to the downtown office.

A portable tent was ordered and set up in one of our guest parking lots, covering what was to become our office.

The portable tent located in our guest parking area quickly became the hub for meetings and lunch.

We started each morning with a team huddle to give the latest updates and work instructions for the day. These meetings helped bring back a little normalcy, as this was an everyday occurrence prior to the storm. It was these simple "stand up" meetings, that became essential to our day-to-day operations throughout the recovery process.

For our team members that need their time away, we did anything we could to remove any guilt and encouraged them to focus on themselves and their families. We knew that everyone would play a major part in our recovery. Fortunately, for the first couple of weeks, we had the honor of having multiple owners and friends stop by to bring our team on property food and drinks. I know our team was so grateful to get a hot meal on a daily basis. I want to thank the multiple owners that were able to donate thousands of dollars in gift cards for our team members in need.

OMAR GONZALEZ, DIRECTOR OF
OPERATIONS

The Aquatics department works hard in clearing a large piece of roof from the pool.

Finally, our first mission of recovery was in full effect; starting the day with stand up at 7:30am, we discussed what the day's mission entailed. We placed all full-time employees into groups in order divide tasks upon team members. Each team had a "lead" ensuring each employee was staying on task and completing their daily goal. Our maintenance team focused on changing batteries on locks for all 210 units on property. This was an essential task that had to been done so that our contracting team could access every condominium to assess the damage from the storm.

Our pool tech lead, Josh Brott, focused on every aspect of restoring the pool. Alongside, our lifeguard team spent multiple days cleaning the pool deck, removing all items making the area an "unsafe" workplace. There is a picture specifically that crosses my mind when I talk about this day.

We had four of our head guards and supervisors pulling a massive piece of roof from building 2 from our lobby pool and pulling insulation with netting before we were able to turn our water pumps on. Our teams took it upon themselves to clean the pool area not knowing how long we would be closed.

Feeding our employees was our next task. There were not many businesses open for our employees to purchase food. Food and Beverage employees and leadership mapped out a plan to provide meals for our employees on a daily basis.

Simple ham, turkey, cheese sandwiches, and salads were provided. After a couple weeks, Signature Group provided us with a food trailer. This later became "Mels on Wheels," after one of our food and beverage managers. Mel later added pizza and salad items to our lunch menu. Being able to take mid-day breaks with all your coworkers surrounding you, was amazing.

Before Hurricane Harvey, while our employees were focused on their own departments, we did not fully understand each departments' roles. However, after just a few days of our team *working as one, we became a family. There were multiple tears shed, multiple smiles exchanged and multiple hugs given. This was a difficult time for each one of us. We all had different tasks but, in the end, we were in this together.*

PAT

CHAPTER 5

SERVICE FIRST

WE QUICKLY REALIZED that we had a new challenge. Metal debris was scattered throughout. Railings were down or wobbly, and flammable seagrass was piled high. Our team members wanted to work, but the property was unsafe. And our contracting teams were focused and in their rhythms.

After the storm, I was with the team that went out to Port A. We didn't know what to expect when we went out there, kinda thought we were gonna pick up some trash and be done. Once we saw we knew it would be a bigger task. Got tetanus shots, and bigger supplies. Went to community center and got direction on where to go. We would get sledge hammers to take out sheet rock, take out carpet, take out fences, transport garbage to the dump, replanted gardens. Literally helped people rebuild their house. People were full of blisters from raking. We did not expect to have that much work. Once we saw how bad it was, not a single soul wanted to turn around. We were all in.

While we were out there, nobody was thinking about their jobs.
The whole group was worried about the family or business that
we were helping. We wanted to preserve the memories from
their homes and take their belongings out as quickly as possible.
We lost track of more time than we could even account for. It
wasn't too stressful, but sometimes you go home in tears. Seeing
the devastation can take a toll on you, seeing that people lost
everything they had. But seeing how happy we were making
people by helping made it so much better.

VIVIEN SANCHEZ, PORT STORE MANAGER

Our next phase started with a simple question. Pat asked, "Do our employees need help?" And we started with Matt Trent's house in Port Aransas. Soon, our teams were helping his neighbors too.

As a leadership team, we thought, "We have two potential problems, and a solution that would work for both." It took some creative explaining to our workers' comp insurance company, but eventually we had permission to formalize our community service efforts.

It was an incredible example of putting our core value of 'Service First' into practice.

The team hangs our values and beliefs on the wall of Impact City Church as a daily reminder of who we are and why we're doing it.

After making the decision to reach out and help those in need of assistance, we met with key members of our leadership team to determine a plan. Taking safety into consideration, we decided to have teams go out together in Port Aransas. These teams consisted of multiple team members, a team lead, and a lifeguard, in case of an emergency.

Our teams were excited for the opportunity to help our community recover and prosper.

PAT

Monday, September 11

9:00am

These were the days that "Port Royal Strong" was truly formed. It became our rallying cry, and also a source of strength in our community.

We didn't just remove trash, and rebuild walls. We helped our neighbors start to rebuild their lives.

We gave each of our employees Port Royal Strong t-shirts so we could easily identify each other. Tetanus shots and safety updates were required too. Our employees loaded into our fifteen passenger vans every day and headed to the community center in Port A to gather a list of residents needing assistance.

The working conditions grew more and more challenging everyday. The damage, heat, no power, and fridges left full of food from before the storm made every location a greater act of service.

I recall a specific story of our team going to a home of an elderly woman in Port Aransas. She had no one to help her. Debris laying in the lawn of her home sent signs to our team to stop and help. This woman's goal was to simply find the urn of her loved one. She was standing there, oblivious to all things around her. The smell was unbearable due to the rotting food that had been left unrefrigerated for weeks. Our team members had to turn just to take a breath and settle their stomachs. Our team took turns digging through the damage, with the goal of finding the missing urn. Finally, after countless hours of searching, the urn had been found. Tears began to run down the cheeks of the woman, and our employees as well.

It was at that moment that our employees knew that they had done something really special.

PAT

One of our volunteer teams set out to help our neighbors in Port Aransas, Texas.

Since day one of Port Royal volunteer experience, it has been more than I expected. Being able to help hands-on gives you an entirely different outlook on the situation. Our first task was with the community center donation project. We did all that we could to ensure we helped get others back on their feet.

Additionally, we cleaned houses that had sewage in them, cleaned the streets, and demolished houses so the residents could start rebuilding. Seeing the difficulty others were having with insurance, made us want to help even more.

BRIAN FRIOU, FACILITIES TEAM MEMBER

Some of our team members showed up to work and serve, even though they were dealing with the impact of the storm personally as well.

It's been a positive impact. I live in the Port Aransas community, so it was difficult to see others I know dealing with something so difficult. On a daily basis, we could all see the impact we were leaving with the city and those in it. People really did appreciate us out there. For one, I became more appreciative for my own situation, even being someone that was affected by Hurricane Harvey. I lost everything. I lost my home. However, I've seen how much worse it can be. So, it's been very spiritual for me.

LUIS VILLARREAL, GUEST SERVICES TEAM

It was such an awesome experience. Going into Port Aransas helping the community, seeing the devastation gave us initiative to volunteer. Some homes had 5-6 feet of water at one point in the storms. Everything was lost. Unfortunately, I had devastation of my own however, there was not much I could do at home until insurance came into effect.

We had such resilient team members. The vision of not giving up lived in every single one of us. Some of our employees being a simple ear to listen to those in need was remarkable. I would look over while throwing trash to see one of our employees crying with a homeowner, sharing stories and hugs. I feel you can look at something like this in two ways.

You can either see this storm as a devastating life change or as an opportunity to change your life. I became such a stronger person after the storm. I was blessed to work alongside my team and community. As many began the volunteer process as showing up to work for a check, that idea changed fast after the passion of helping someone overtook us all. For those of us working on property, there was nobody there to help us but us.

We are all in this together.

SABRINA GRUBBS, AQUATICS MANAGER

Having employees that knew exactly what others in the community were going through helped them overcome their own challenges. After deciding to extend our workplace and not confining our employees to our property, the responses received from the community made it worth the long hours and "out of the ordinary" working conditions.

Being in Port A seeing the multiple home and families torn apart made me want to do something to help. It looked like a war zone when we first visited the community. Trash and pieces of people's homes laid in the streets. Port Royal gave us the opportunity to help others. I had never gone through something so devastating as Harvey and, when I was asked to return to property, I knew we needed to work fast. There was a lot to be done in such a short period of time. We are getting through it. It will take us time to be completely finished. However, I know we will overcome this hurdle.

CHAD TIFFANY, FACILITIES TEAM MEMBER

Going out and volunteering really hit home. The home owners in the community were thankful. That's what kept us going, helping others. Appreciation from everyone in the town brought many smiles and tears. It was rough. It was hot, but we pushed through to help. No matter the situation we were in ourselves, all put aside, we were there to help.

JOHN GRANT, POOL TECHNICIAN

October 3, 2017

Being in the community allowed us to make connections with our neighbors, and also many businesses and organizations. Our team members spent countless days at Heavenly Hope Center of Port Aransas working alongside Lisa and her team.

Hey Port Royal team, this is Lisa with Heavenly Hope! I don't know if you've been here to shop, but you know we had a lot of debris and our property was just crazy. Today, we had a team from Port Royal here to help us. They showed up, and now they are sweaty. They are amazing! Thank you all so much for everything you have done for us. Ensuring the safety for our shoppers is our main priority and, you helped us achieve that goal. Your bosses at Port Royal are rockstars and again, we want to say thank you.

LISA MCCLELLAN, HEAVENLY HOPE
CENTER OF PORT ARANSAS

Our teams help community members sweep debris, nails and
metal from driveways and parking lots.

October 11, 2017

Eventually, our community service efforts broadened to meet
new challenges brought on by the hurricane.

First, the Coastal Bend Food Bank needed extra help creating
bundles of food for families that were impacted by the storm. We
dedicated a group of employees to assist, and those employees

became an extension of their daily operations team for many months.

Many of our other staff members were used by local organizations, such as the Corpus Christi Food Bank.

The Coastal Bend Food Bank relied on our team members for 1,068 hours of volunteer services, averaging $9,612 that would have been paid to warehouse employees. We helped prepare 67,284 meals for families around the Coastal Bend area, and volunteered 728 hours at Habitat 4 Humanity Restore.

SARAH PEREZ, HR COORDINATOR

Our teams also served at the Salvation Army, The Women's Shelter, Dress for Success, Habitat for Humanity, Texas State Aquarium, and multiple other community organizations.

The first Friday at The Salvation Army was a challenge. We were not sure they would be able to accommodate the many generous team members willing and able to participate. They were excited and thankful that we had such a large group willing to help. After anxiously waiting an entire day, we heard back from Yamid, the Volunteer Coordinator, with the message, "Thank you so much for all your help, they were amazing." It was wonderful and uplifting to hear those words and we knew this was a huge step for our team.

Next, we collaborated with Habitat for Humanity. The first day we helped with the restoration of a home. This was a good experience for our employees. A few days later our team was sent to "Habitat for Humanity Restore" and they returned with a lot of feedback. The positive energy from the Habitat for Humanity team trickled down to our team members, making it one of their favorite places to serve. Sorting, taking inventory, and organizing has proven to be a truly rewarding experience.

Something special came out of the work we did at the Food Bank. After multiple months and long hours of volunteer services provided, we were told Cecilia Abbott was making a trip to Corpus Christi to see the impact of the Food Bank firsthand. It wasn't until the day of Mrs. Abbott's arrival did we get more exciting news. Not only was the Governor's wife planning on visiting, but Karen Pence, the wife of Vice President Mike Pence along with Melania Trump, the First Lady of the United States, were also joining on the trip to Corpus Christi.

All three ladies made their route viewing the devastation in Rockport, Port Aransas, and surrounding areas. Upon their arrival to the Food Bank, First Lady Melania Trump wanted to know how we were involved. Our Director of Human Resources, Pat Bell, had the opportunity to explain to Mrs. Trump exactly what our teams were doing to assist after the storm and the importance of community involvement.

SARAH

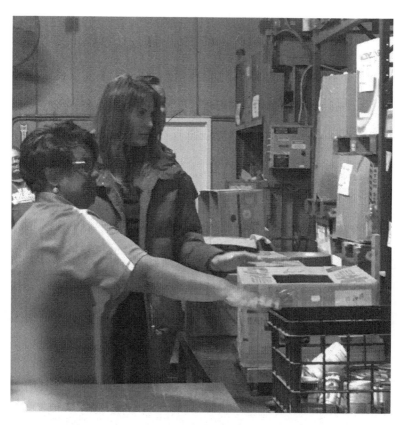

Pat Bell meets with First Lady Melania Trump at the Corpus Christi Food Bank to explain what our teams have been helping to accomplish.

From an administrative perspective, our community service efforts added all sorts of challenges. Our HR team rose to the challenge.

That was really an interesting process, we learned a lot from trial and error. At first we had everyone on a spreadsheet in alphabetical order and put an X by their name, that indicated whether they were present for work. As we started sending people to various locations, it became critical that we knew exactly where everyone was at, so we would have the entire team meet at the church in the morning and sign-in for a specific location. This made my job easy, because it helped me determine who I could send to a specific location. It is not as simple as saying "ten people go to the salvation army, and twenty to the food bank." You really have to try and cater to each employee's need, whether it be a ride or a special accommodation. If it were up to our team, they would all be volunteering at the same place. Once we had our team meeting, employees were released to their designated locations, where they would have a team leader call and confirm that everyone made it safely. After I had that confirmation, I would put the information into our attendance spreadsheet, and either myself or Brent would travel from different locations to make sure that everyone was okay. We really wanted to stay in touch with the managers of each location, because we wanted a strong working relationship with each partner.

SARAH

To most people, the meaning of Port Royal Strong is about our journey through the hurricane. To our teams, it has come to mean so much more.

All of our lives have been changed forever; all in ways we have never imagined. It has been amazing to see what was ugly devastation turn into the beauty of growth and strength.

The opportunity to be a part of a bigger cause, and help those in need was such a rewarding and satisfying experience. Not only were our teams helping the community, but they were reshaping their perspective about their own recovery.

PAT

The volunteer experience was tiring but, also so rewarding. The entire time we were out there, I kept thinking 'If it were me in this situation, I would appreciate the help.' When other government organizations could not help in a timely manner, there we were to help in any way we could. Seeing homeowners' personal items destroyed and thrown away made us want to help even more. Being able to see the impact we were leaving in the community; the thanks and hugs I received every day made it worth the long days and hard work coming home every day.

JOE DEASES, GUEST SERVICES
SUPERVISOR

We not only helped remove debris and reconstruct homes in Port A. We served hundreds of people at the Salvation Army, help provide meal boxes for hundreds of families with the Coastal Bend Food Bank and, assist in home building with Habitat with Humanity. With the Salvation Army, we helped in their kitchen as well as their store. In addition, we helped Dress for Success move locations. At Habitat for Humanity we helped build homes. We were one of the only consistent group of volunteers that showed up every day. Most members of the community needed the help, and we were there for them. Our Port Royal Strong shirts really meant something in the community. Everyone knew what we were doing. We were there to help.

SARAH

CHAPTER 6

CREATING OUR UNIVERSITY

AS WE MOVED THROUGH SEPTEMBER, we had a few new insights. We realized the pace of recovery was going to be much longer than expected - by several months. We had dozens of team members that had been impacted and would be coming back soon. Some team members were working on property, lots more were serving throughout the community, and our administrative team had relocated downtown. We were incredibly spread out and needed to find new ways to stay connected.

We talked to our Board and sought as much counsel as we could, but eventually came right back to our values. 'Keep Getting Better' was a value we had adopted many years ago. The one thing we did have was time for training. I asked Pat to create a comprehensive training program, and Port Royal University was born.

After a few weeks of our employees pouring their efforts into the community, we realized that our timeline to return to Port Royal would be several months away. Then it became real that Harvey had given us a great opportunity that many companies don't experience - a time to pause and invest in our employees through training.

PAT

Passport to the Future

Port Royal team members meet to kick off our new Port Royal University journey.

The Port Royal HR Team is festive in their cruise attire.

On October 8, we had a kickoff party at Schlitterbahn to share the plan with our team members. We used the theme of a passport to represent the journey we were about to begin.

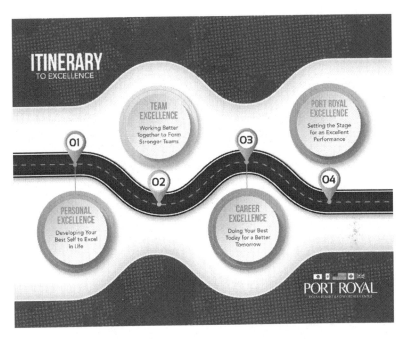

Our team members were presented with the itinerary that would guide us through our training program.

Our four destinations for focus were:

- Personal Excellence – Bringing the best you to work
- Team Excellence – Working together to form a stronger team
- Career Excellence – Doing your best today for a better tomorrow
- Port Royal Excellence – Setting the stage for an excellent performance on property

Thankfully, Impact City Church allowed us to use their sanctuary each week for our training center. Our beginning sessions included goal setting, financial wellness, a health care fair, mental wellness, and vision boards. We realized that many of our employees had never taken the time for personal reflection. We used "The Success Principles" by Jack Canfield as our textbook.

We had several guest speakers including Port Royal Owner Bill Mann, Liza Wisner from City of Corpus Christi Training Center, the Charlie's Place team, Sean Olivares, and a heartwarming visit from the Mayor of Port Aransas.

During personal excellence, our team members learned how to:

- Take 100% responsibility
- Stop excuses, blaming, or complaining
- Choose their mindset: Event + Response = Outcome
- Decide what they want
- Start the 7 steps of Financial Peace: $1,000 emergency fund
- Remember their healthy choices and next steps
- Set a Wallet Goal

Sean Olivares leads Port Royal University through an important message about being our best.

One thing I learned from Port Royal University is that you must take 100% accountability of your actions. You can not look for anyone to blame; you must look in the mirror. My favorite part of the training program was watching the video of Eric Thomas' motivational speech. It really hit me right in the heart. You can make time or you can make an excuse.

JOHN REYES, CONTROLLER

Kendra Kinnison addresses the team about our weekly teachings
from the Success Principles book.

At first we thought it was something to eat up and waste time to
be completely honest, but after learning everything we did in
each aspect, the training program was awesome. I did not
expect to have as much fun as I did learning, listening to the
guest speakers, and the activities. The idea from Bill Mann and
his wallet goals stuck with me. I was able to follow through my
goals, even until this day. I've always listened to the Dave
Ramsey shows and it had the same theme. I related to the
stories Mr. Mann spoke about with his kids. The group breakout
sessions Pat ran was a good experience. The lifeboat lesson had
a cool perspective of the priorities each of us had and what was
necessary.

DONALD SMITH, FACILITIES TEAM MEMBER

Bill Mann, Owner at Port Royal, teaches some of the key techniques our teams can use to become financially stable.

During the duration of PR university, I gained knowledge of many concepts and principles. The one that I have been able to follow through with is the idea of wallet goals from Bill Mann, one of our board members. Mr. Mann challenged us to save $83 from every paycheck to reach the $1,000 goal after six months. I decided I wanted to double Mr. Mann's request. Not only was I able to reach my goal but, I have not stopped contributing to my emergency fund. A weight loss challenge was another idea that was introduced to our team. Those of us that were interested in participating in the weight loss journey were paired in teams.

BRANDON CROWSON

Volunteer experience was great for me. Not only did it give me a chance to help others, but myself as well. I don't really handle crisis very well, so keeping my body and mind busy was great. During Port Royal University, being less educated school wise, it gave me the heart to learn more, to be a better person. How to help others as well as myself was my main goal. I've never worked for a company that wanted to help their employees grow whether it be here or at any other company - financial, personal, team. How to handle myself in the public eye is one that I learned. I actually still have every piece of paper that was given during the training program. I have learned to become natural. Mr. Mann stood out to me. I did not know about paying myself first. I learned how to communicate with others by Liza. Communication issues for me has been a problem. Being able to talk to others that may not be in the same "class" as your status, stood out to me. Port Royal has been the best company I have worked for and, I am not just saying that. Anything I can do to help my company, coworkers, and guests, I will put in my 100%. That is why I come to work everyday. That's my job; that's what I love to do.

CURTIS GOODE, FACILITIES TEAM MEMBER

Team members work through different exercises and worksheets
during the Port Royal University program.

Pre-Boarding

At the beginning of our training program, we gave our employees
the opportunity to pick a different journey. We knew there were
some folks that were not comfortable with the rebuilding
process. It was inherently messy and often uncomfortable.

To ensure that folks understood our seriousness, we offered a
'quit bonus' of two weeks pay. We gave them a week to think
about it, and provided a discrete way for them to let HR know of
their decision. No questions asked, and they would be eligible for
rehire when we reopened. Four team members took the offer.

. . .

For those that decided to stay, we asked them to think about what they were 'packing' for our journey ahead. Some items we suggested were a commitment to yourself and our team, a growth mindset, and the willingness to learn about new tools needed for success.

We did have engaged, disengaged and actively disengaged team members. Some simply could not understand the decisions that were made or did not want to follow them. I described our engaged employees as those who wanted to improve their contribution level, wanted to sharpen skills/knowledge, and understood why they came to work everyday. The disengaged employees were those who just want to do their job without any extra effort. The actively disengaged employees were those who didn't want to be there and tried to discourage other employees from giving their best.

We did not want to have the Harvey victim mentality. We did not want to be defined by Harvey (event) but rather our response, which would be Port Royal at our rebuilt phase. We asked our employees to look in the mirror. If you don't like your outcomes, change your responses. Now was the time to focus on what we could control versus what had happened to us.

PAT

Continuing to Learn

From the personal excellence section, most team members created a 'wallet goal' to focus on until it is accomplished.

. . .

Nine employees committed to GED classes. Others added a variety of personal and professional classes at the Texas Workforce Center such as Excel and Personal Leadership, English as a Second Language, and a driving class.

It was beautiful to watch our teams' pride and confidence grow with each week's lessons. We could see the benefits extending to other areas of their lives.

Employees were encouraged through interactive trainings throughout Port Royal University.

Watching the video from the Navy Admiral gave a good insight on starting your day by making your bed. Unfortunately, I have to get up at 5:00am every morning to make it to work on time. On my days off, I woke up early and made my bed to start my day. I know I gave my 110% during this time of recovery. I always give my best every day, for the past 26 years. There is only three housekeeping supervisors so, we all have to work together to complete the daily tasks. I noticed during team excellence the importance of teamwork. I saw how much harder my team worked after going through the training program. We all worked as one. Instead of team members questioning authority, they have stepped up and took on extra tasks everyday. We are the Port Royal family. In times of desperate needs, we all work together as a team now. We did not associate with other employees outside of our department until this training program. It was such a great experience.

ROSA FIELDER, HOUSEKEEPING
SUPERVISOR

Liza Wisner joined us during Port Royal University to share her background, and tips on being successful.

I have been able to follow through with my wallet goal. I was able to be apart of the courses at Workforce Solutions inside Sunrise Mall here in Corpus. During the week course, I learned about resumes, customer service, and Excel. It was a great experience. We had some other team members working at the Dress for Success so, we were able to eat lunch with them every day. It was nice seeing that our employer really cared about us. Being able to expand our minds and education was a good opportunity.

ELAINE BROOKS, F&B SUPERVISOR

The Texas State Aquarium hosted our teams for a holiday luncheon where our teams heard appreciation from our community partners

For Christmas, the Texas State Aquarium thanked our employees by hosting us for a wonderful luncheon and then gave us the day to enjoy the Aquarium. Our partner community organizations were also there to share the impacts of our team's service. Our employees could hear firsthand that they had made a difference. It was the perfect way to pause and celebrate our journey.

Personal Excellence was interesting for me. I have been through a Dave Ramsey course multiple years ago. However, I took Bill Mann's advice for wallet goals to heart. After the storm, I knew there was going to be some financial debts in the near future. The motivation kept me going. I knew how the system worked, I just needed the drive. I knew financial troubles were coming soon from my home damages and rebuilding. After consolidating multiple credit cards, we have paid off most of our credit card debts. We are on one last card paying off. Adding more to my emergency fund was a great choice. Putting away $75 from each paycheck into a separate account at a completely different bank that I normally use. I still have my wallet goal in my wallet; someday I will get there.

SABRINA GRUBBS, AQUATICS MANAGER

The Port Royal Aquatics team does training off-site while the pool
at Port Royal is restored.

CHAPTER 7

LEADERSHIP BOOTCAMP

AS WE RECOGNIZED the growth in our team members, we realized there was another important area of our organization that we needed to invest in as well - our leadership team. These are the folks that truly operate our resort on a day-to-day basis. For our progress to be lasting, our leaders would be the key.

In mid-December, I challenged Pat to transition our University curriculum to start the new year. Our team members would need to concentrate on community service or external personal training programs. And our leaders would have the time and support to prepare us for re-opening.

Alignment

Our first focus was to get alignment on the responsibilities at each level of our organization. In the past, we'd often been stuck in figuring out who could make a decision or solve a problem.

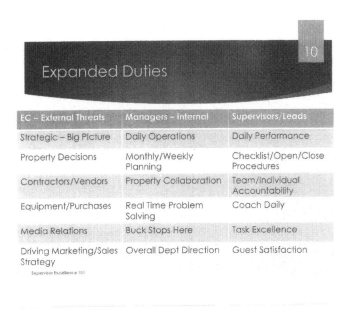

Expanded Duties

10

EC – External Threats	Managers – Internal	Supervisors/Leads
Strategic – Big Picture	Daily Operations	Daily Performance
Property Decisions	Monthly/Weekly Planning	Checklist/Open/Close Procedures
Contractors/Vendors	Property Collaboration	Team/Individual Accountability
Equipment/Purchases	Real Time Problem Solving	Coach Daily
Media Relations	Buck Stops Here	Task Excellence
Driving Marketing/Sales Strategy	Overall Dept Direction	Guest Satisfaction

Supervisor Excellence 101

Separating our duties by executive committee, managers, and supervisors/leads helped our teams understand the functions of each role in the company.

In our organization, myself and our five Directors are part of the Executive Committee. We're tasked with our guiding our overall strategy, making major property decisions, external stakeholder communications, purchasing, media relations, and designing our marketing/sales plans. Our management team is responsible for daily operations and real time problem-solving.

This explicit expectation to make decisions was an important understanding and shift, and it took some time to flesh out. For this approach to work, our managers would need to feel supported and to trust themselves and each other.

When we started the leadership bootcamp, I was confused honestly. I wasn't able to understand exactly what Pat was wanting us to do. After multiple weeks, I was able to see the opportunity and lessons we learned I have been able to utilize with my team. I have become a better leader for my department. Having the confidence with my job role and the knowledge of procedures and checklists that were taught to us gave me the opportunity to go further with my team and supervisors. We were able to change our own departments to run more efficiently. When Pat had guest speakers, I felt the management team was able to use those conversations in the leadership bootcamp. I, myself, got a lot out of the training program. I did not feel confident to begin with. I was able to participate and ask questions instead of sitting back. Being able to open up with our team changed my perspective of teamwork.

Managers before the training were basically walking on eggshells. We were scared to say anything to higher managers in fear of responses we would receive. Being given the authority to run this property the way we wanted without having to ask for permission has given us the ability to do what we all need to do in order to make Port Royal a place for our guest to create memories to last a lifetime. I see the leadership team stronger now. We are able to solve problems without having to ask for help. However, when we all need help, we have the ability to escalate issues and questions to our superiors when needed without any hesitation.

There has been a lot of communication between us managers

this past year that has made us stronger. We want to thrive and make our property better in the long run.

HILDA CANTU, HOUSEKEEPING MANAGER

Being able to talk to other managers that had held their position for multiple years was great. The ability to discuss different scenarios with other management team members was the best part of it. We learned multiple skills in leadership but, mainly we learned how to work together.

ERNIE TIPTON, FACILITIES PROJECTS MANAGER

Village Leadership

One key discussion area that emerged from these first weeks of Bootcamp were the non-negotiables that our managers decided were important standards to have across all departments.

Leadership Bootcamp was a safe zone. Our management team was able to put our heads together, sharing ideas of items that we could continue practicing and items that we no longer needed to do. For instance, our tardy grace for our employees was not an easy conversation to have. We came up with that. Several of us noticed that many employees in the past had been taking advantage of that situation. We had a problem, and together we found a solution.

SABRINA GRUBBS, AQUATICS MANAGER

We adopted the term 'village leadership' to reflect our shared responsibility and teamwork. This helped reinforce a collective approach to leading our team members.

PAT BELL, DIRECTOR OF HR

Re-Imagine

Next, our managers had the opportunity to re-imagine their departments - rethinking our structure, updating job descriptions, clarifying new roles, and identifying any gaps that needed attention.

We found out that some of our checklists work, and some do not. Instead of having one long checklist of everything that has to be done, we are breaking it into increments. Using group checklists, each group will have a specific duty to do for that given week, all completed with multiple members of the team. Having the ability to spend time training with my guards has been beneficial and quickly became a new priority in my mind.

SABRINA

One of my favorite days was when the managers presented their new mission statements and key action items. They clearly supported each other, and understood the key handoffs between departments. I was also inspired by their growing confidence.

We went over a lot of planning for the upcoming season along with teamwork skills. It was great being able to work with the other managers in an open forum. We had to present the plans, vision statement, dress codes, non-negotiables, and training ideas to the Executive Committee. We had the ability to run property and make decisions on more sensitive information than before. As the season went on, we were able to handle more situations on our own. We all felt more comfortable however, it was a challenging. It took multiple conversations and exercises with myself to stay sane. Communication is the major takeaway from the manager bootcamp. There was so much that wouldn't be able to accomplish without communicating with one another. Overall, I believe it was a great character building program. I am more confident and mentally and emotionally stronger.

TYE WEST, GUEST SERVICES MANAGER

CHAPTER 8

15 MINUTES TO SPARE

EARLY IN OUR RECOVERY, we focused on being open in April and May for our school groups. We knew it would be incredibly challenging. Perhaps on the verge of impossible.

We also knew that there were few places for large groups to stay, and if we weren't open, they likely wouldn't be able to participate in their competitions. Everyone who could have cancelled already had.

We mapped out the game plan from mid-January forward, and tracked our progress each week to ensure we were on schedule. In addition to repairing and furnishing our rooms, we'd also need to restore our pool and solve the puzzle of foodservice operations.

It was intense, exhausting, and required an incredible level of teamwork.

Not long before groups arrived did we get electricity into the units. There we a lot of rush orders, so we ordered extra furniture and ended up really needing it. It was very hectic and sometimes felt disorganized, but we took it one step at a time. We all worked long days, sometimes into the night, and it was exhausting but exciting too because we were going to have people here again. Wilcox Furniture was a great help to us. If we needed something, they got it to us that day or the next. Amy and Eric just stepped right up and got us whatever we needed.

DEB FUESSEL, OWNER TEAM

Seeing the long-time employees' dedication on property made me want to work two times harder. There were multiple weeks of lifting heavy furniture and throwing away items. Doing all that in the heat outside was rough. Seeing others doing the job nobody ever wants to do made me stay and show up to work every morning. My team became my family. Port Royal is my second home. We had to get this place up and running again. I knew my team very well, I couldn't walk away and leave them behind. This is really a beautiful place, not only the buildings, but also the people.

CHAD TIFFANY, FACILITIES TEAM

Tye West, Front Desk Manager and Melissa Dixon, Reservations Manager both help the housekeeping team throughout the days leading up to our first guests.

We were worn out. The heat, mosquitos, and rigorous work began to finally take its toll. We returned to the tent area and noticed bins of sandwiches waiting for us. It had been almost four or five months of eating the same ham and cheese, turkey and cheese, and pizza every day. However, there was a surprise waiting for us all. A peanut butter and jelly sandwich. And oh goodness, was that sandwich amazing. It brought me back to my childhood. That one simple addition to our day kept us going. It's silly, I know. But that one simple sandwich helped us push through the day. We all worked together as a family. I knew I was part of making Port Royal the best it has ever been.

RENEE TILLEY, HOUSEKEEPING
SUPERVISOR

The Fountain at the pool was welcomed by all teams and inspired us to not give up.

We pulled the roof out of the pool and had to use water pumps to circulate the water from the lobby pool all the way to the top pool. We had to vacuum everything, and we had to get all the debris from the roofs out of the filters so they could filter properly.

When the pool was done, we felt accomplished. From what it looked like after the storm to being clear and swim-able was a great feeling. We knew that we had something to show for all the hard work we had done, being able to look over and say "I helped bring this back to life."

JOHN GRANT, POOL TECH

The pool area nearly completed gave our employees a little "taste of normal" during a challenging time.

As we inched towards the deadline, we realized just how close it was going to be. Had the groups been able to stay anywhere else, we certainly would have made that choice. But we didn't want to let the kids down. And having a firm date on the calendar gave us a very specific date to aim for - April 5.

We were completely transparent with our Board and the group leaders.

Sunday, March 25

I sent this update to share our status and next steps.

Board Members -

I wanted to keep you all informed with where we are now. It's intense.

We will partially open and resume operations on April 5 with about 50-60 rooms ready. We have school groups contracted, and the rest of the city is sold out as well. The same is true for the April 12 weekend. When it became clear that there was no turning back, the contracting team rallied and found a path forward.

We're well into the final push, with our teams and contractors working from sunrise to sundown every day. Our first meeting is at 6:30am, and then we have stand up at 7:15 and have teams in their work areas by 7:45am. Each day, it's very tightly coordinated with AmTech, Signature Group, and all of their subcontractors.

We are altering our plans and will be focusing on completing Building 3 before we move to Building 6. (This updated timeline will be the focus of the next owner update.) It became clear that the workflow for the crane, curbs, and AC systems needed to be on one side, and then move to the other, as opposed to alternating back and forth.

We have passed the framing, electrical, and plumbing inspections for Buildings 4/5, and for 17-24 on Building 3. We have the next round of inspections for 9-16 on Tuesday. Completing these allows us to close up the drywall and begin the "finishing" process of texturing, painting, deep cleaning, staging, etc.

We are working aggressively on the elevators and believe that they will pass inspection before April 5. If not, we will provide alternative measures while occupied.

We passed our inspection on the food truck and have our sales tax permit. We will begin food service operations before April 5.

In short, it is bumpy and imperfect, but we will re-open on schedule. And the imperfections will continue to be addressed each week until they are resolved. I don't know that I have the words to express the level of effort and dedication that this requires from each of our contractors and our teams. There is something very special happening here.

I am working on the next owner email with updated timelines, and will continue to provide updates every few days. I am generally working from my truck on property, so communication is a bit more challenging.

I hope you're all proud of the path we've taken through this. I do feel like I'm walking the plank right now, with no possibility of turning back. The only option is to keep moving forward and figure it out each step of the way. Thankfully, the teams have embraced the goal with the same dedication.

This has been a tremendous experience, but hopefully not one we'll need to repeat again anytime soon.

kk

Our Sales Team was also in constant contact with their groups.

In the weeks leading up to the group arrivals, I was in constant communication with my groups, because I wanted to be straightforward and let them know well in advance what the state of the property was.

ERIN TODD, SALES TEAM

There had to be some really serious conversations with our contracted groups about the state of our property and checking if they still wanted to come. We wanted to give them all of the information and let them make the decision on whether to come or not.

RUBY ACUNA, SALES TEAM

From: **Erin Todd** *<etodd@port-royal.com>*
  Date: Fri, May 4, 2018 at 1:24 PM
  Subject: Port Royal - Property Update

As mentioned before we will still be under construction on some parts of the property. These construction areas will be gated off and secured, but please watch your step around the property. I have also attached a few pictures of the property to give you a good idea of where we are and how far we have come. Please see my notes for some of the pictures below:

Pool View From Slides

Port Royal Entrance - upon your arrival this is the current state of our arrival area

Construction Area (Main Building) - this is of our main building which is the one TOTAL rebuild building. The only accessible area for this building will be our open air Plaza where guests will be able to enjoy food from our food truck.

Each condominium has been touched in one way or another. Every condominium has received a new AC, however this means the ceilings in the kitchens were taken apart in order to get to the refrigerant lines. Therefore, in order for us to open our doors in time to our groups these ceilings were patched, but remain unpainted. You may also find in some condos the flooring incomplete, but we have done our best to lay rugs. Some condos may also have unfinished walls with only the drywall up.

Pool hours during your stay:
   Sunday, May 20th 7am-11pm
   Monday, May 21st 7am-11pm
   Tuesday, May 22nd 7am-11pm

The pools are open and also the designated path for you to get to your condo and the plaza where the food truck is. Lastly, in place of Restaurant 361, we will be offering food truck service. I have attached the menu for this service.

Just keep in mind we wouldn't open our doors to our groups if the condominiums and property weren't safe and secure. We are thrilled to have your group apart of our story! I highly recommend sharing this email with all of your chaperones, so they are aware of our property's status before their arrival as well.

Please let me if you have any questions about this information, and I am happy to help!

Cheers,

Erin Todd, Sales Manager

To make matters even more challenging, we had another storm blow through on Wednesday, March 28, that handed us a few extra curveballs. Our construction team quickly regrouped to keep us on schedule.

Wednesday, April 4

For the last few weeks, we had been working in tight coordination with City Inspectors. As soon as our contractors completed an element, they were on-site to inspect.

At 7:30pm on Wednesday evening, we had a planning call to be sure we were all clear on the final items that needed attention before we allowed guests to return. We each made our lists and committed to stay in contact throughout the day.

Thursday, April 5

When the day finally came, I remember feeling nervous and excited, almost overwhelmingly so. But I knew I'd need to hold myself together if we were going to ask our teams to stay focused.

<u>*5:27am*</u>

I sent an update to our Executive Team.

Okay, here we go ....

There are still several challenges to be overcome today, but I think we have a solid chance of making it through the gauntlet. It will be intense, and it will likely require each of us to take point on key areas.

Coordinating with inspectors will be my primary focus, and I'll need Bonney to assist as the Safety Plan is a key point. I expect we'll have a large contingency from the City on site as early as 7am.

Noack - I think we need you to take point on the guest experience outside of rooms. We need to make sure the Building 2 area flows and is setup well, and that we're not missing any obvious details in the pool area or entrance.

MShack and Omar - we need y'all to stay on point with rooms, particularly Building 3. Lots still needs to happen today. The flooring folks are getting started at 6am and expect it will take 12 hours to finish all the rooms. We'll need to have our teams move the furniture. Paul should have the list of the rooms they're starting with.

Pat - we need you to be home base and shepherd the Board and any other visitors we get today. It's possible the media may show up. During lunch, I'm thinking the flow may relocate to the gathering space in Building 2.

And we'll likely need employees to stay late to finish a variety of projects. Helping to facilitate that as they emerge will be helpful.

Let's also start making notes of employees and teams going above and beyond. There are certainly plenty of folks giving us incredible effort, and we want to be sure and recognize them in all the appropriate ways.

Let's just keep steady and hang in there. I do not believe
God got us this far to come up short today. I have faith that
we can navigate whatever we will face today. I love you
guys. Let's do this.

kk

The day was just as intense for our contracting team. They were
as committed as our internal teams.

---

*It was a very stressful day. We had very lofty goals. With some
of the conditions we were facing, it was a challenge. We knew
Port Royal had contracted groups, and we had to meet our
goals. Everyone bought into it and was there helping out.*

DAVID VINSON, AMTECH SOLUTIONS

4:15pm

After receiving all green reports on our other inspections, the last
open item was the report from the Fire Marshall. We'd worked
through his previous list, and he'd arrived earlier in the afternoon
to conduct another inspection. He was firm and thorough, as
we'd all expect. But I couldn't help feeling the intensity as the
minutes ticked by.

. . .

After a meeting with David and our Safety Team, he gave his approval at 4:15pm.

4:30pm

15 minutes later, the first bus with students from Prairie Lea High School arrived. I'm certain they passed each other on Highway 361. I remember fighting back tears as the students stepped off the bus.

Prairie Lea High School helped motivate our teams and showed their support by wearing our Port Royal Strong shirts during their stay.

I was walking condos myself to make sure they were fine. The rest of the property wasn't quite perfect, so I wanted the condos to be as good as they could be. I swept the patios, picked up tools, and got trash out of hallways - all while they were pulling in.

The elevators weren't ready yet so we had to help everyone carry up all of their luggage. They were troopers and the sweetest kids. They understood everything.

ERIN TODD

But our day was far from over. We were open and had checked in our first guests. But several busses from Klein High School were still on their way. Thankfully, they would be arriving late, so we had a few more hours to keep working.

8:30pm

We ordered dozens of pizzas and took a break for dinner. As we called everyone down from the floors, we realized just how many team members had stayed. Even several of our Board members were helping to clean hallways and finish putting furniture together.

Our teams rallied for a late dinner before getting back to work to welcome our first guests back to property.

1:00am

Oh my God. That was the day we stayed until 1am. I was ready to fall down and cry. The teams were exhausted, but thankfully we had life guards, FM, and even Accounting helping us. It was just chaos. Most of the kids were just exhausted from the long bus ride, just happy to get in their rooms. They couldn't wait to get out to the pool - they were excited. It was aggravating because we were there so late. We were doing everything we needed to do to get them ready. It was a rough day.

We survived, got everything done, left here around 1:30am and then we came back at 7am the next morning. We serviced all rooms for trash and towels, but only the chaperones got full service. Some of the chaperones were upset but we kept smiles on our faces. While they were out for band activities, we continued working on their rooms. By the second night, they understood that we were still under construction and how hard we had worked to get even this far. On our end, we were just excited that they were here and they knew that we were doing our best. It was overwhelming, but we made the best of it.

HILDA CANTU, HOUSEKEEPING MANAGER

Friday, April 6

We were exhausted, but giddy. David and I recorded an update video:

Kendra: *So it is Friday, April 6th, and this is hands down the favorite video we've ever done. We're standing here looking back at the pool area with dozens of kiddos having fun. We are officially open and serving our contracted groups. We're just so proud and excited to have been able to meet the deadline. I'm going to share a little bit about the folks that made that possible. We're honored that they still chose to come and be our first guests, and we know we're in great shape to see all of our* *families and friends starting June 1st. So David, tell us a little bit about all that we accomplished yesterday.*

David: *First of all, I gotta tell you, it feels great to be in the position we're in. And to have such a great team a part of this project - without the help of the City, Development Services, our Port Royal team, our contracting team it would have never been possible. We have an incredible team. And we were able to make our goal and we have these rooms occupied by these groups and it is a great experience to be able to see people having fun out here.*

Kendra: *So we're about 25% of our rooms open.*

David: *Yeah and that's just the first part. I mean we're at 25% and we're already starting in on the next phase. So this thing is not going to stop until we get every one of them behind us. We're going to have more of these victories.*

Kendra: *Honestly, we're a little wiped out - it's been a lot of late nights and a lot of around the clock for every trade that we've had. Oh my goodness, from roofers to building envelope folks to our electricians to our plumbers to our gardeners, our AC contractors, of course [Amtech], Signature Group, our Port Royal team - we had a meeting in this space last night and we all came down to grab a quick bite before the last hurrah about 8:30 or so - there was probably about 85 people here. It was a special night - certainly a day we'll never forget. We were in this space when we had called our team back on September 5th, the first day after the storm that the majority of our team came back. We were in a very damaged building. And then last night, that same team rallying to make it happen.*

So we've still got a long way to go - our rooms are safe and secure, but not as pretty as we'd like them to be. Still a lot of paint and trim and things like that to be taken care of. But we've got a couple of months to make that happen, and a lot of groups helping us to get back in rhythm. It's a great day at Port Royal, it's a great day for Mustang Island, and for all the folks in Corpus Christi and Port Aransas that have cheered us on - we're excited to continue this journey. And David, thanks so much for all that you've done to get us to this point.

David Vinson, Kendra Kinnison, and Rian Glasscock shoot a video for our guests and owners about our opening days.

Saturday, April 7

Our teams continued working throughout the weekend to make their stay as comfortable as possible. Unfortunately, the dust from so much new sheetrock just kept re-appearing as it settled.

Thankfully, the group leaders understood the full context and stayed in constant communication with us.

We'd also planned to host a pool party for them as an extra thank you for being our first guests. But the weather wasn't cooperating. It was cold and rainy.

We didn't want to cancel, but we didn't have any other options on our property. We called our friends at Schlitterbahn, and they saved the day. They allowed us to bring the DJ and the pizzas and allow the kids to use their space for the party. It turned out fabulous.

Mayor Joe McComb presents the Key to the City to the Band Director of Klein High School.

Corpus Christi Mayor Joe McComb also came by to welcome the group and give their band director a key to the City. The kids were so excited. I don't think there was a dry eye in the room.

It was an incredible moment, and I will always be grateful for their understanding and support. I know it wasn't easy to be the first guests back after a hurricane, but they played a pivotal role in our recovery. There will always be a special place in our hearts for Prairie Lea and Klein High Schools.

Throughout April and May, several other school groups joined us in the adventure of hurricane recovery. Construction was ongoing, and the weather was often unpredictable. Thankfully, most were as resilient and positive as our teams. We did all we could to make their trips special, sponsoring visits to the Aquarium and USS Lexington and sharing lots of pizza parties and t-shirts.

As the Director of South Coast Music Festivals for over 30 years, there have been 2 events that had a major impact on the festival and its student participants. The first was Swine Flu and the second was Hurricane Harvey. Swine flu wiped out one week of the festival and no schools were permitted to travel. Hurricane Harvey's effect lingers on with a resolution as yet undetermined. Through both events, Ruby Acuna and the staff at Port Royal have taken the lead in making sure the students were able to reschedule or be accommodated whenever possible without penalty. Port Royal is a big part of the student experience and thus a big part of the festival. They have been and continue to be a great partner as I strive to provide a rewarding and fun trip for the music students in Texas and beyond.

PAUL DAVIS, SOUTH COAST MUSIC
FESTIVALS

Hi Erin - our group had a great time and your staff was amazing. In fact, we were just talking about next year and making plans to return.

I know our boosters have posted on facebook and I hope they were able to tag your facility. You guys did a great job getting things in order for us.

I do look forward to talking again soon about next year.

DAMON VELA, MUSIC DIRECTOR • LORENA
I.S.D.

We've always treasured and looked forward to the visits from our school groups each year. Now, even more so. Those that cheered us on during this difficult time will be permanent VIP's at Port Royal. Their support and encouragement became our fuel.

CHAPTER 9

OPENING DAY DISAPPOINTMENTS

Friday, May 25

We shared this video update with our owners, team, and guests. Despite our best efforts, it was clear that we were going to come up short.

Nine months ago today was a time at Port Royal that I don't think any of us are likely to forget. It's a bit ironic that today is a Friday, and that August day was a Friday as Hurricane Harvey strengthened into a Category 4 and made landfall very near us. I think we knew as soon as we walked outside the next morning that the journey back would be lengthy. We've heard from others in the industry and the recovery business that one to two years is often how long things like that take.

As we regrouped in those first six to eight weeks, and talked with our owners, our team, and our guests and our construction crews, we set - honestly - what was a very aggressive goal. We set that goal back in October. You could say it was right on the edge of impossible. But we're okay with being on that edge. We feel like we owe that level of effort and commitment to our teams, to our owners, and certainly to our guests. You tell us how much you love coming to the coast and coming to the pool, so we want to have that ready for you just as soon as we can.

So we've got some good news and some not-so-good news. I'll start with the great news - a week from today on Friday, June 1st, we will reopen. We will be ready for families. Our pool area is in amazing shape. Our rooms, for the most part, look great. We've even managed to set up an event center and lots of food and beverage options to accommodate all the fun stuff you want to do on property. We have an amazing calendar of events planned. It will be an awesome summer at Port Royal.

The not-so-good news is we're not where we want to be in terms of the number of rooms that we're going to have available next Friday. Our construction teams came to us at the end of last week and said that we couldn't quite make the schedule. There have just been a few curveballs here in the last few weeks that we just couldn't make it over in time to hit June 1st. We think we're only going to miss by two to three weeks, and we think it's going to be about 30% of the rooms that we had planned to have ready.

So - what does this mean for you? If you're a guest and you have a reservation for those first few weeks in June, or really any time in June, if it's possible for you to move your vacation to later in the summer, that would be fantastic. We will honor your rates, just email or call our reservations team and they'll take care of that for you. If you don't call us, we'll probably be calling you for many of our guests.

And, if you're sensitive to the experience, you may want to come later in the summer. We will still be doing some elements of construction - more in those first few weeks of the summer than later. From time to time, it could be a little bit noisy if we're finishing up our roof or something like that. You know, landscaping and those finishing touches - those will be still going on. So if you're particularly sensitive to the experience, again, a little bit later would be better. If you want to see what hurricane recovery looks like and be a part of that - maybe go volunteer at Port Aransas or Rockport or other areas, then come on down. You'll get an authentic view of what being a part of hurricane recovery looks like. We'll certainly share any information you'd like to know about our experience. We know lots of folks are just curious how that has worked.

It has been an incredibly intense nine months. I don't think our teams or our construction contractors could have worked any harder. If hard work and intention alone could get it done, we'd be done. But unfortunately, weather, materials, and sequencing - there are just some things we can't completely control.

For owners, we'll have more information for you in our weekly email and in the owner portal. We do know that you want to get back in too and you want to make some of those finishing touches, and again - we'll be in touch with that detailed information. But know that we're thinking about you too. We know you want to be back home and back to having it just perfect for guests, and we want that too.

We also just really want to thank the groups that have started visiting us in April and May, and I have to say - Prairie Lea and Klein High School, you'll always be in our hearts for being the first to let us get back in rhythm. You've been fantastic at tolerating our construction. And hopefully us getting opened enabled you to participate in the events when the city was otherwise sold out. We just want to thank you for being a part of the story - you're forever part of those chapters. And one of the things that you've shared with us that we know that we need to let everyone else know - driving on to property right now, the first impression isn't the greatest.

Unfortunately, our lobby building, building 2, took the brunt of the storm. The worst part of the storm came from that bayside. And so that building is not available at all right now, and looks a little bit intimidating. But know that right behind that building is a fully thriving resort, beautiful pool area, and we think you'll be pleased at the way we've been able to creatively solve some of the challenges and give you a preview of what's in store with a brand new redesigned building 2 with first grade amenities and great features.

So bear with us on the first impression. Know that our teams have filled in with a lot of heart. Anything where the facility is not perfect, know that there is a team member standing by to more than make up for what's not right. We think you'll be really pleased with the way our teams have taken Service First to heart.

We invite you for the summer at Port Royal. Again, work with our reservations team on the specifics and if you can give us just a little bit more time, we would appreciate that too. But we will see you this summer at Port Royal.

Then, we planned an All-Hands meeting with our team at 2pm.

I thought, WTF. I just couldn't believe we were going to have to cancel that many people. We started by preparing our team. We gathered the information we needed: guest reservations and spreadsheets, then divided them up amongst the team members. We prepped them on what to say and how to say it, but it's easier said than done. It's much harder to actually make yourself do it. We were trying to stay professional and knowledgeable, even though we didn't have all the information we needed. The guests had a lot of questions. It wasn't just one guest - but hundreds and many yelled at our team, because they didn't understand that we had been destroyed by a hurricane nor the recovery process. Those who understood felt sorry for us.

MELISSA DIXON, RESERVATIONS MANAGER

I felt more bad for the team that took the brunt of the work, it was pure frustration. All guests' summer vacation plans were extremely important to them, and you feel guilty ruining that for them. Not taking it personally is very difficult when they're crying or yelling at you. There was nowhere else they could go - nowhere else was open. There are days you wake up in the morning that you just don't want to do it.

SARAH ZIEGLAR, RESERVATIONS
SUPERVISOR

Leading a team through that - it was hard. We jumped on the calls too, because that's the only thing we could do to make it better. We tried to stay positive and, of course, we all had our days. It was very damaging to the morale in the department. It never got easier, even though we had to do it day after day.

We stayed in communication with Front Desk regarding room availability. Kendra and Pat talked to the team one day when they were falling apart and tried to make them feel better. It's easy for our employees to think everyone else is sitting there with their feet up and wonder why they are the ones who had to make the cancellation calls. It can be easy to lose perspective and remember that everyone is working on different aspects of hurricane recovery.

MELISSA

On one hand, we wanted to celebrate. We had worked as intensely and aggressively as possible since the days before the storm, and there was significant progress. We would be re-opening. Hundreds of families would be able to enjoy their summer vacations, and we would be contributing to our community that relies on tourists to support their restaurants and other businesses.

On the other hand, we didn't meet our estimates for the number of rooms we would have ready. Lots of folks were rightfully upset. And our team took the brunt of those conversations. We were getting skewered on social media too.

It was brutal. I felt like I'd failed my team - that I'd set us up for failure. I questioned whether I was the right leader to finish the project, but I knew that didn't matter in this moment. I drug myself out of bed each morning committed to have as many conversations as I could, hoping that any upset person I spoke with would be one less person for the team to hear from.

We literally took it one day at a time.

Friday, June 1

Before we knew it, opening day was here. I didn't feel ready or comfortable, but we just kept going, taking it one step and one interaction at a time.

I tried to thread the needle in our communications, sharing

kudos to the teams that had worked incredibly hard, and also being sensitive to the folks that were disappointed in us. It was hard to find the right words for a message that captured the duality of how we felt.

We hold our first stand up meeting the morning of
June 1st, planning the arrival of our first guests.

Today is a testament to resilience, teamwork, faith, courage, and a spirit of service. Today, we celebrate a critical milestone and the accomplishment of our main goal - to provide an opportunity for families to make memories to last a lifetime.

Just like everyone else impacted by this storm, we're a long way from the finish line. We know there's still plenty of work to be done.

Landfall was just the beginning. The challenges have been

non-stop ever since. Often, it felt impossible and hopeless. Many times, we debated whether we should give up on our goal for this summer.

But we're built to serve. It's who we are and what we do. And we're ready to serve families today, though not quite as many as we'd hoped.

For the folks that are mad and disappointed, we understand. We are too. We've given everything we've had for nine months and seven days, and there were still obstacles we couldn't overcome. If it's possible, we still hope to see you this summer. We appreciate your grace and understanding.

We're not perfect, but we are Port Royal Strong. We've worked incredibly hard to have our house ready for you this summer, and we hope you'll come to see us.

June 1 - it was a good day. It was stressful, super stressful. But we made it happen. All of our guys, you could see the pride in their eyes that we made it happen. They felt prepared and more confident that we could control the situation.

ERNIE TIPTON, FACILITIES PROJECTS
MANAGER

It was different opening on June 1st than it was in April. At least with the school groups you communicated with one person. With regular guests we try and communicate but they still have pre-Harvey expectations. A lot still expected more than what we had to offer. Not all of our condos are perfect but we try to offer activities outside, and we try using discounts as well. Anyone at the front desk can give a discount, and we have a compensation guide based on what you could offer. All based on what the agent views appropriate in that situation. I created a "hot sauce guide" to help determine the level of compensation based on the situation and the guest. It explains the different levels (mild, medium, or hot) and what you should offer.

TYE WEST, GUEST SERVICES MANAGER

It felt like we were more prepared, and it was definitely different. One of the biggest changes was to have the Event Center and Front Desk instead of just the black trailer. It was nice to get back to reality.

For the most part, guests were understanding of our situation. Repeat guests are different than new guests. Usually, our new guests were more difficult. Their expectations didn't meet reality. Through this experience I learned to look at every situation as what I would want for me and my family. From my perspective, what would I want in this situation? Then that is what I try to give to guests.

CRYSTA STUART, GUEST SERVICES
REPRESENTATIVE

Our Marketing, Reservations, and Front Desk Teams also worked together to update the messages we shared with guests before their arrival. Again, we wanted folks to be excited about their vacations, and we also wanted to be honest about the recovery process.

Hey there,

We wanted to send a quick message to let you know how excited we are that you're coming to stay with us during our very first weekend back since Hurricane Harvey made his unwelcome visit in August through the Coastal Bend.

Since August, our teams, contractors, and our community have been working hard to help Port Royal recover from the storm. It's certainly been all hands on deck. All the sacrifice and countless hours have led us to this day - our biggest milestone. We are finally welcoming families back on the property. This is not the end of the recovery journey for us. We still have a road ahead of us leading to more exciting milestones, like a fully renovated main building.

Welcoming families this year will be a little different than previous years. Please don't be alarmed. We have worked through and thought of just about everything to ensure you and your family have an excellent experience despite the temporary changes. Below you'll find exactly what you should expect upon arriving at Port Royal.

Welcome Station: Upon arrival please stop at our welcome station, where our friendly guard will greet you and help you find your way to our check-in station.

Check-In Process: Our dedicated front desk staff will have a mobile check-in process at the circle located in front of our main building. This will allow for faster check-in and avoid long lines at the temporary front desk area. A guest service agent and supervisor will be available at the temporary front desk area, located in the Event Center, for further assistance, questions, or concerns.

Parking: Upon check-in, our staff will direct you to your parking space. Parking is limited at the moment, so any off-property guests will need to follow parking directions provided by our welcome station.

Main Building: As we've openly shared on social media and previous emails, our main building is currently not available for rooms and may look a little scary. Behind the main building, you will find a thriving resort full of life, our gorgeous pool, and staff with huge smiles ready to help meet your needs. At the first floor of the main building, you will also find the Plaza, where you can enjoy food from our Port Royal Strong Food Truck and relax under the shade and enjoy the breeze.

Food & Beverage: Because of the hurricane, we lost Restaurant 361 and the Bistro, which were located in the main building. During your stay, we will definitely have some great food options available. A temporary setting for Restaurant 361 will be located inside the Event Center (the big white tent). Our friendly servers will be ready to serve you from our 361 Mobile Kitchen menu which includes breakfast, lunch, and dinner. Under the Plaza, you will also find the Port Royal Strong Food Truck ready to serve you a quick meal. The menu looks a lot like what you would enjoy at The Bistro. Due to the limited storage space, food will not be served on china or glassware.

Cabana Bar: Our Cabana Bar, located poolside, will be available for guests to use. Our contractors are currently putting the finishing touches to allow us to serve you your favorite cold adult beverage.

Rooms: Rooms are coming along great. Some condos still need some finishing touches. None of these finishing touches are hazardous. Rooms are fully air-conditioned, clean, have internet and are safe for you and your family. In your room, you could find the possibility of a wall with mismatched paint or primer, missing trim around doors or baseboards, or an Amazon Fire Stick instead of cable due to unprecedented challenges with wiring

Please know we are working on those finishing touches as

diligently as possible. We will continue to work until every single unit meets Port Royal excellence at 100%.

While you're here, our team has scheduled family-friendly activities for guests of all ages to enjoy. We hope you enjoy our resort and all the fun activities happening during your stay!

If you have any questions about any of the events or regarding your reservation, please don't hesitate to call one of our reservations specialists at 1-800-242-1034 or press "front desk" from your room for the Front Desk.

Travel safe and we'll see you soon,

Martha Knight

Martha Knight, Marketing Manager
Port Royal Ocean Resort

Thursday, June 7

Our guest interactions were starting to improve.

After opening day everything was definitely different - it wasn't dealing with just one group, but individual parties that had their own problems. We were still under construction, not many people were happy about it. Cable, AC, etc. were issues. We helped them out as much as we could. In most of the rooms we had fire sticks for cable, so most of the requests were, "Can you fix my TV?" The strangest request I received was to clean 3 building hallway because there were dead fish in there. Someone went fishing and decided to leave everything they caught in the hallway.

We did what we could to make up for what we didn't have.

It was nice when guests started to realize that we're still recovering.They were more accepting of our strange accommodations. People are getting used to the idea that we're doing the best we can with what we have. If a room is missing blinds, furniture - we move them around. Go up with carts, pack up, move as fast as possible, and some people are so appreciative of that.

DALTON WOMBLE, GUEST SERVICES
AGENT

Board -

Thought I would share this comment and Melissa's reaction.

Helen Edwards Seriously, EVERYONE is killing themselves to get more rooms ready. One elevator did not work for most of the time and the workers were not used to having guests stay so it was frustrating to have them park in our parking space because we did not want to park in someone else's. The poor front desk workers were like valet managers....move this car there and this one here. BUT THE GOT IT DONE. And with a VERY cheerful attitude. Based on the devastation that we saw at some of the other properties it was apparent that Port Royal really is #PortRoyalStrong. If you have not been to Rockport or Port A you won't believe just how hard hit they REALLY were. Try to make another date later in the summer work for you if you did not get in this week. The Dive In Movie was great. We will be back next year for sure. Stay with it #PortRoyalStrong. And keep those cheerful happy people on staff. They were awesome.

Love · Reply · Message · 13h

I don't have words to tell you how hard this is on all of us - far harder than after the storm. But we are in it together, and we are making progress every day.

It fuels us when owners or guests acknowledge that in a positive way. This team is special.

kk

Email from Melissa Dixon
   RE: Facebook Comment
   June 7, 8:37am

Literally brought tears to my eyes!

That was much needed for everyone and I am definitely sharing this with my team.

Thank you for sharing!

Friday, June 8

We knew we had to keep communicating and share another video update.

Good morning from Port Royal. It's Friday, June 8th, and we have officially survived our first week of being reopened. It's hot and sweaty, and an exciting day.

I wanted to share with you and tell you a little bit more about how the last few weeks have been for us. We know that many of you are frankly disappointed and mad at us and feel like we ruined your summer vacations, and that breaks our heart. That was certainly never our intent. The whole point of getting reopened as quickly as possible was so that families could come and enjoy their vacations here. So I want to share a few things with you.

First, it has not been from a lack of effort. Literally since the day before the hurricane, we have been working hard to make sure we can recover as fully and as quickly as possible. We took a little time off at Thanksgiving and Christmas and it's honestly been nonstop ever since. About May 18th we had our first indication from contractors that a critical path item just wasn't quite on schedule and they were going to regroup and let us know where we were with that June 1st deadline and that same weekend that they were working to regroup, we had a heavy rainfall - Sunday, May 20th, just hit us at a very vulnerable time. It was almost like a very mini hurricane, but in terms of the sequence of events that we had to run through there was quite a bit of recovery that was needed and we lost that week of planning to that week of recovery.

And now we were at the 25th and really getting a handle that we were going to be down a whole building. And really the experience in that building, even if we had been able to open a few rooms - was not going to be a good one. And so we made the decision to go ahead and not open that building immediately and give our contractors time to bring it online in a healthy and safe way.

It's not something that we've known about for a long time. We've always known that our schedule was tight. There wasn't a lot of room. There's a reason these recoveries take years and not months.

We've pushed everybody to the absolute edge of possibility to make this happen, and for the most part there's a lot that's gone right. We did come up shorter than we wanted to and there's nobody on our team that feels good about that or takes that lightly or doesn't realize the impact that has on families.

So we hope that you can reschedule and join us later in the summer. If those dates are fixed, if you have family coming in from out of town that can't be rescheduled we hope you'll join other properties nearby that are open. Our community needs tourism. For Port Aransas and Padre Island, tourism is a big driver in the economy - it supports jobs, it supports a lot of things. And so part of our getting reopened - and lots of folks getting reopened - is to keep those jobs and support the economy. So we hope you can understand the spirit with which we've tried to recover from the hurricane, even if we haven't been perfect.

We've also had some folks get upset when we share positive pictures of people having fun by the pool or positive pictures of progress. And again, we don't share that to be offensive or rub it in or make anyone feel bad that they're not here.

But know that we need to celebrate too - our teams, our contractors - lots of folks have been working incredibly hard - around the clock in many cases - and away from home. Lots of our contractors have been away from home for nine or ten months now. That's a really challenging thing.

Lots of our team members still don't even have their homes repaired, and they're still showing up to serve our guests every day.

We are in this for our families and our guests, but we need to celebrate too to be able to keep going.

So please, let us find the joy where we can - join with us in the joy. When we come up short, contact us. We will do everything we can to make it right. And we'll keep working hard until we do make it right.

We appreciate you, we appreciate your faith in us, and we hope that we make you proud. Thanks so much.

Friday, June 15

Within a few weeks, we were starting to get in rhythm. And then we saw the weather forecast.

The rains in May were heart wrenching. I took it extremely personally. Everyone was depending on us to assess the building, protect it, and keep further damage from occurring. From that point forward, I vowed to double efforts and give it everything I have so that doesn't happen again.

If we could have put a giant tent over Port Royal, we would have. We did preventative repairs and then other repairs on top of those. You have to be ahead of everything. You have to be prepared and have a Plan A, Plan B, etc. and think of every scenario possible. And you have to have the team. Kendra, Rian, and I were able to take on any path, no matter what the direction or starting point.

DAVID VINSON

Email from David to Kendra

RE: Weekend rain forecast plan & action items taken to minimize risk of water intrusion

June 15, 12:14pm

Kendra,

Looking at the forecasted rain from today through Tuesday next week, Amtech and Signature group have made preparations to have equipment and manpower in place should we have units with water intrusion. As you know Amtech and Signature Group have a plan in place to take action should it be necessary. Specifically, Amtech will be a liaison between Port Royal, Signature Group, and other contractors. Fernando will be working with Port Royal guest services staff and Port Royal Management to relay and distribute communications to the appropriate contractors. Shawn will be in the field to help expedite action items should they be needed. In addition, we will also have small crews available through the weekend from Rio Roofing and Plumbers.

To date the following action items have been taken to minimize the risk of water intrusion:

1. Temporary roof coating of the above attic space in Buildings 3 & 6
2. Installed temporary roof drains above every unit in Building 3 & 6. Storm water drainage is piped beyond the footprint of the building.
3. Temporary scuppers installed where roof has been demolished to help alleviate storm water.
4. Visqueen installed behind parapet plywood.
5. Visqueen installed over parapet plywood and composite lumber cap.
6. Ice and Water shield membrane installed in shingle

fashion over the interior, exposed stud wall. Base of the membrane is sealed directly to the concrete deck.

7. Ice and Water shield membrane installed over curb flange

8. Ice and Water shield membrane and sealant of corner transitions where roof has been demolished.

9. Sealed base track of metal stud framing above buildings 3 & 6.

10. Roof mounted curb drains have been plumbed with storm water being piped beyond the footprint of the building.

11. Curb penetrations have all been temporarily covered and sealed.

12. All roof penetrations have been sealed and resealed.

13. TPO Temporary roof installed over all 3rd floor water heater closets where the roof has been removed.

14. All debris from the roof attic space has been removed to ensure drainage of storm water.

15. Temporary exterior wall coating of Building 4, 5, & 6

16. Temporary exterior wall coating of breezeway walls in Building 3

17. Seal around all exterior windows in Buildings 3, 4, 5, & 6

18. Building 3 & 6 sealant above balcony stucco wall transition

19. Temporary coating of breezeway base wall in Building 6.

20. Temporary coating of breezeway base wall in Building 3 (in progress today)

21. Hydrojet of all breezeway drains in Buildings 3 & 6 to remove all debris.

22. Sump pumps hooked up and placed in the above attic spaces to remove water where roof has been demolished.

23. Plumbed balcony drains on second and third floors to extend beyond the footprint of the Buildings
24. 3 coursed with elastomeric and fabric at water heater closet base.
25. Sealed and re-secured temporary roofing above water heater closets
26. Installing 2 part acrylic coating at base of balcony stucco walls and doors (in progress)
27. Daily reminders to contractors to keep the building watertight at the end of each day.

David P. Vinson, MBA - Project Manager

Between June 19-22, it rained 15 inches on Mustang Island. It was painful to watch, and to face the effects of every morning. Just as we started to find our rhythm, we knew there would be more cancellations.

Our teams simply kept at it, one day at a time.

The rains over the summer were frustrating. Lots of rooms got flooded, and it was like, "here we go again." Yet at the same time, we had done this before so we knew we'd get through it. We've been through worse. That gives you some perspective that it's going to be okay. Yeah, there are some problems and it will take a while to fix, but not nearly as bad as the Harvey damage.

DEB FUESSEL, OWNER TEAM

We've learned that your expectations can't be fixed because there are so many unknowns. Things change on a daily basis. It was hard because we were used to planning months ahead and our team had to adapt to planning daily.

This has been a learning process for all of us - I think in a good way. It made us closer as a team - all having to be on the same page at the same time. Going through it together forced us to support each other instead of just complain. You can voice frustration, but there's no one who will solve the problem for you. It helps when everyone is going through the same things you are.

MELISSA DIXON

CHAPTER 10

BUILDING MOMENTUM

RAIN POPPED up in the forecast the night of July 4th. We all held our breath.

At 6am the next morning, we regrouped to assess. Thankfully, our temporary repairs held.

Later that same morning, I savored the view from the pool area. The atmosphere was great. People were loving life and enjoying their time at Port Royal - both guests and our team members.

I could see that our work and dreams had come to life.

The Plaza at Port Royal used to be our Grand Ballroom, but is currently a shaded area with nice seating and plenty of games for families to enjoy.

Thursday, July 5

We shared our next video update.

We've been operational for right about a month now. First and foremost, I want to say we're sorry to the folks we've had to reschedule or in some cases, cancel or move to different places. This journey to recovery has been full of twists and turns and new weather surprises.

The hurricane was unfortunately the first of many storms - thankfully none quite as extreme, but two weeks ago, having 15-16 inches of rain was another twist that I don't think any of us saw coming, and we had to deal with.

Thanks so much for your patience and understanding, and I think if you come down to the area, you'll understand what a struggle it is and how committed we are to being back to a place where you can make memories to last a lifetime with your family.

And for the folks who have been able to join us here - thank you too for your understanding and your patience. We are a little bit different property. The pool area is as fantastic as ever - hopefully even more so with our new inflatables and other adventures.

But our rooms are very much still a work in progress. While we're thankful that they are safe and secure, they certainly need some paint. We're still working on our roof. Our contractors are working as discreetly and as quietly as they can, but again a challenge to keep that construction going and keep making us stronger so that rain and things like that don't disrupt us as much.

We're all celebrating this morning that it rained last night and it was not nearly as disruptive as it has been in the past, so we've made some progress. And also, not nearly 16 inches, so thankfully just a regular rainfall and all of our regular drainage systems could keep up with that.

I hope you all had a wonderful Fourth of July with your families. We're so thankful for the folks who were here to celebrate with us. And we've got several more weeks of summer so if you've still got time for a summer vacation, fit us in and we'd love to have you.

I started working at Port Royal on June 4th. It was an interesting time because we had just reopened and everyone was working hard to accommodate our guests and figure out the "new normal." One of my job responsibilities is to plan the activities calendar for each month. So I booked live music, sandcastle lessons, yoga, Zumba, and dive-in movies for the month. We also decided to make the 4th of July really special. So we decorated the cabanas with bunting, hosted potato sack races, passed out popsicles around the pool, and Food & Beverage set up a free hot dog bar for guests. After hosting those activities on property, the Sales team and I went out to where they do the fireworks show in Port Aransas. We worked with Jackfish Rentals to get a golf cart and put some Port Royal banners on it. Then we drove around and passed out fans, glow sticks, and sunglasses to everyone out there. We just wanted to show our support for the community and let everyone know that Port Royal is back up and running. That was a fun day. It was long, but it was fun. I loved the way our teams came together to bring joy and help make memories for our guests.

KALEY O'BRIEN, MARKETING & EVENT
COORDINATOR

Power of the Plaza

The plaza is a great example of how we'd begun to think differently about our property. We'd lost our lobby, ballroom, and food service areas. But we recognized some opportunities too.

*In 2 building, the first floor was demolished to use it as an
assembly area. We gutted the whole bottom floor because it was
so damaged and there was safety concerns. We made the most
of it by polishing concrete and removing walls, and getting rid
of the safety issues. The city allowed us to have a permit and
occupy the site. It was an opportunity to change the look of
Port Royal.*

DAVID VINSON, AMTECH SOLUTIONS

The #PortRoyalStrong wall became the centerpiece of the plaza.
It's everything we've stood for throughout this journey.

*Shortly after I started, I was sitting in the Plaza with Erin
having lunch. We were talking about the property and the idea
came up to paint the wall in the Plaza. At the time, it was just
white and had drywall glue all over it. So we brought it up at a*

meeting with our teams, and everyone seemed excited about it. We all brainstormed other things that we could do with the Plaza, and developed a vision for creating the space that we now have. Martha, Erin, and I got to work on removing the drywall glue from the wall and painting it. It took a long time - it was a lot of work, but we finally completed it. We also removed the paint that was peeling from the pillars and painted those white. Even just doing that changed the whole space. Then we ordered some lounge furniture and giant games. It turned out awesome. As soon as we got it finished, guests were there playing games and lounging almost all the time.

We painted the #PORTROYALSTRONG letters on the wall as the finishing touch. For me, this area really was a symbol of that. We took what was originally just the bottom floor of a destroyed building and made the best of it. It was by no means perfect or ideal, but we made the best of what we had. Looking around property, you could see that happening everywhere. I was proud to be on a team like that.

KALEY

Families staying with us joined in to support our teams by not only wearing their Port Royal Strong shirts, but customizing them.

This is the time where I felt the most team work I've ever felt at Port Royal. We went out to buy the paint, materials. We painted the wall. We bought games. First we had to scrape the wall. That was not as much fun. Then we painted it and put #PORTROYALSTRONG because we wanted it to be a symbol of our strength and to use it as a place for families take pictures. It's been successful ever since. That's one of the things guests

comment on most in our reviews. People really enjoy it and get
excited about it. We had it all finished by Fourth of July.

MARTHA KNIGHT, MARKETING MANAGER

In addition to our guests, team members took time to take
photos in front of the wall.

One of our key phrases is event + response = outcome. I don't
know that we fully understood that when we learned it during
Port Royal University. But now I believe we really do
understand that events don't define us, our responses do. And
we've lived through that. We've embraced change, focusing on

the things we can control. To be honest, the Plaza area is an example of that. It's now a place for us to celebrate, enjoy, and appreciate.

PAT

We added some floating obstacle courses to the pool area to give our guests even more amenities.

Throughout the summer, we continued to have activities. We added poolside s'mores on some weekends, which was a huge hit. Families loved to come gather around the fire pit to cook s'mores. Kids had a blast with it because they got to roast their own marshmallows, eat their s'mores, then go jump back in the pool.

KALEY

We knew we weren't perfect, but we tried everything to ensure all guests had a great time - such as stores by the pool.

I think having activities has really taken us from surviving to thriving. We have to figure out how to thrive in our new environment because this is our reality for a while. We have to find those bright spots, even though we don't have everything we want. When we create better experiences for guests, we create better experiences for employees, and they realize how they contribute to the guest experience. I have to say, I'm really proud to be a part of that.

PAT

Guests gather in our heated pool to watch a movie during our Dive in Movie events.

Lots of guests enjoy the dive-in movies. We love to be able to put it out there. I love seeing the happy, smiling faces. S'mores has been one of my favorite activities to do so far because we are able to be out there and interact with guests. As soon as pit goes out, people come out and ask when it's going to be ready. It's one of the best things for me because I get to see people out there having a great time. Most times we run out of supplies. It's a good problem to have because people are enjoying it so much. Guests enjoy the games at the Plaza. I go every hour or two hours to fix everything up because people use them so much.

DALTON WOMBLE, GUEST SERVICES

Families love learning techniques to building sand castles on the beach with Mark Landrum.

I think it was really great that we were able to bring back more activities than we have done in the past. We've always had a lot of those activities, but never so many. It brought about a lot of teamwork and that was awesome. I had never been so hands on with stuff before so it was a lot of fun.

MARTHA

The Anniversary

On August 25, 2018, we gathered together again.

Texas State Representative Todd Hunter speaks at the "Port Royal Strong" one year anniversary event at Port Royal Ocean Resort.

For those who don't know me, Port Royal is in my district. I'm the legislator that has Port Royal. Hurricane Harvey hit on August 25th. On the 26th, which was actually Saturday last year - the Mayor of Port Aransas could not get in to Port Aransas because in front of your units were downed poles - electric lines. And it took bulldozers to clear the highway up here so Port A residents and everybody up and down this highway could get back and forth. And there was no cell service - no internet. Anything.

Now, Kendra..Kendra called me just a couple of days - and the problem, everybody, is you can't see Port Royal and the condo units from this roadway. So she called me, I came right over and it looked like a bomb blew up. And at that time still nobody really knew what had happened. And if it hadn't been for her, myself and others would not have seen what had occurred - because you can't see. And when she called, we tried to help. But it's because of your folks that we knew and we helped...And if

*you can't get a postcard that Port Royal is coming back look
right out there at the pool. There is nothing better.*

*I have a saying...in South Texas, the coastal zone - it's,
"Trabajando juntos hacemos las cosas. Working together, we get
things done." And what better place to kick it off than
Port Royal?*

*What I did to send a positive kickoff - is we flew over the capitol
a Lone Star flag in honor of Port Royal. And here's the most
important thing - this is a Lone Star flag - that means
something. This was flown in your honor and on behalf of Port
Royal. Congratulations, thank you. Thanks for all the good
work. And staff of Port Royal - keep it up!*

STATE REPRESENTATIVE TODD HUNTER

Corpus Christi Mayor Joe McComb shares his experience of his
first time coming to Port Royal after the storm.

It was a pretty eye opening experience - obviously coming back this way, following the hurricane. And you realize that it had been a pretty devastating event. And as Todd mentioned - really, if you drive from Corpus now over here - it looks great coming down the highway now, and the only thing you see is a bunch of new telephone poles or power poles. So you know something's up because they don't change those out very often. So you realize what the devastation was. When you turned onto 361 - the poles were at about a 30 degree angle, you got a little further down, they were at about a 45 degree angle, you drive a little further, they were across the road so you realize the devastation we had gone through.

Port Royal isn't really just announcing today that they're back...I have a daughter in law, a son, a granddaughter, and a grandson, in Houston - Spring, Texas. And every year for 25 years I guess they bring the band down to Port Royal for a weekend trip. And the band director says, "we're not going to Corpus if we can't go to Port Royal." This was in April. Well, I'll tell you - they worked their fingernails off and whatever else they worked off. And they told him, "we will be ready for you if you bring your kids down here so we can let the world know that we're open and ready for business." So in April, they brought 600 or 700 kids down and Port Royal handled them back in April. So they've been working hard to get this thing up and running. And I want to commend you for that. I came out - got to see them, that was great...they had a great time. Port Royal has been working like Trojans to get back up and the spirit was great.

We've come a long way. The spirit of Texas is not going to be quenched by a hurricane...We are looking to better days ahead. The Scripture says that "weeping endures for the night, but joy comes in the morning." I can tell you from personal experience - this experience and others - that there's a new day dawning in

South Texas and Corpus Christi, and I'm proud to be part of it, proud to be your Mayor. And congratulations to you for getting it back up and running. And I truly believe that our best days are ahead of us, and it's because of folks like you.

JOE MCCOMB, MAYOR OF CORPUS CHRISTI

Port Royal Board President Jerry Ellis speaks about our journey to getting open for our Spring school groups.

We had contracts with those groups at this resort, and have had those contracts for many years. The high school kids - they've grown up down here, and they work very hard until their Junior or Senior year, and those band members come to competition every year in Corpus. It's great for our economy, it's great for Port Royal. And we had those contracts, and we wanted to honor those contracts...I can tell you...we didn't have the Fire Marshal's pass through until 15 minutes before our guests - we had 15 minutes, we got it, and the busses started arriving. So it was because of the leadership in Corpus and helping us get to that point to honor those contracts. And we didn't have every one of these rooms available, but we put those kids up...the pool was beautiful and they enjoyed it. So, thank you, Mayor.

Most of you know her, but Kendra has led our team members and Port Royal. I'm excited for her to share with you a little bit of the journey. I'm just, I'm amazed and I'm grateful for what you've done and how far you've brought us.

JERRY ELLIS, BOARD PRESIDENT OF PORT
ROYAL

General Manager, Kendra Kinnison, recognizes and thanks all of the teams, contractors, and community members that have made this possible.

Thank you. Definitely a better August 25th than the last one. Although, it didn't get real until the 27th or 28th. Thank you for all being here. You're all here for a reason, and today, many of you are our guests of honor...I hope our owners and our team members, and we've got a few guests here today, and lots of folks from the community - I hope the thread that everyone realizes is what a team effort this was. Certainly, for the Port Royal team, and our contracting team, and our owner team, and our board team, but so many other folks have been on our team this last year.

We did open April 5th...it was ugly. There's really no other word for it. It was rough. We were here for a very long time - well into April 6th, I think. But a long day. Each of those weekends in April and May - it was tough. That first weekend, it got cold and they were supposed to have a pool party and we ended up at Schlitterbahn. They let us have their room. We had ordered pizza, they let us bring the pizza in. They were just amazing to us.

I came across a - I think it's Latin - Amor Fati - a saying that I read again the other day. I think the specific translation is "a love of fate" but I think the broader interpretation is "to love all that happens." And I don't know that I can love all that's happened with Harvey, but I think I can love how big our family has become. I think the Port Royal family and my family has definitely expanded this past year and it's awesome to be here with you all today, together to celebrate...we've come a long way.

Again, thank you all so much for being here today, and for your support all throughout the year.

To Bryan Stone and Daniel Carlisle, our attorney and insurance agent – you helped us plan and prepare for when this day would inevitably come. And you were on the ground with us just days after when it did.

To our Board – you rallied with us just hours after the storm had passed, helping us to decide on next steps, and know that we were supported. You've been right there with us, guiding each step of the way.

To Amtech Solutions – We didn't even have to call. David Vinson, you were here by Monday morning, coordinating with David Day, and ensuring that structurally we were safe. To this day, you've never left. The level of commitment and dedication that you've shown to Port Royal is beyond words, and we appreciate it more than we can express. Thank you to Architect Mike Hovar, and new Corpus Christi office GM David Vinson. James, Fernando, and the entire team, we appreciate you too.

To Signature Group – You were our first miracle. After a chance meeting with Daniel as you were about to leave town, you were on site by Sunday evening and gearing up by Monday morning. You guys knew how to make an entrance – diesel generators and an entire power distribution system, climatization equipment, and an army of folks and machinery to get us stabilized. Then you pivoted to continue to provide construction leadership and navigate all the other 'fun' weather and insurance challenges that we've had since. Special thanks to Rian Glasscock, and Project Manager Mark Bice. We've always been partial to blue, but we have to say that orange is quickly becoming our favorite color too.

To the City of Corpus Christi Development Services – You've been our partner all along the way, guiding us through each phase. You all helped us break the project down into solvable components, and you've worked diligently and timely, often inspecting at precise moments, just between when the work was complete and guests were arriving. I remember our 8pm phone conferences to get through key milestones. City Manager Keith Selman, and Development Services leadership Nina Nixon-Mendez, Gene Delauro, Bill Green, and the teams that worked with Yvette Dodd and Isaac Perez. I know there's probably not a team member in the entire floor that hasn't helped us. We thank you, and we ask for your continued guidance throughout the rest of our recovery, particularly in this building here.

To APS Security and Wilcox Furniture, other key vendor partners that have kept us moving forward. You've been there for us literally every day, protecting our property around the clock, and delivering appliances and furniture to get us back up and running. We know our 'terms' are laughable, and we appreciate your patience with us. Baldemar Saenz with APS, and George Moore and Crista Parra with Wilcox Furniture, we appreciate you so much.

To all the community organizations that allowed our employees to serve with them last fall and spring – Port Aransas Chamber, Habitat for Humanity, Charlie's Place, Metro Ministries, the Food Bank, Dress for Success, Salvation Army, Purple Door, North Padre Watch, the Texas State Aquarium, and the Art Museum. You gave our employees a home, lots of love and support, and a positive mindset. We know this was only the beginning of our work together, and that we're forever joined in a spirit of service to this community.

To Impact City Church – for allowing us to use your sanctuary as headquarters for Port Royal University. Pastor Felix Trevino and your team, we appreciate your love and support during our toughest months. You, too, helped our teams feel at home.

To the Texas State Aquarium for hosting our team Christmas party and helping us with loose ends on opening day. Tom, Jennifer, and the team, we appreciate you. We're still talking about those amazing grilled cheese sandwiches, and having the afternoon to explore all the exhibits. It was a beautiful escape from tough times.

To the hotels and travel partners that helped us navigate a very bumpy April, May, and June – Emerald Beach, Holiday Inn on the Island, Schlitterbahn Corpus Christi, and Beth Owens in Port Aransas for helping us work through all sorts of creative challenges.

To the Texas Travel Industry Association Board of Directors and COO Dan Decker – thank you for being our first group in June and all your encouragement. And Dan, thank you for bringing your care packages early in September. Your visit lifted our spirits.

To the Corpus Christi CVB and the Port Aransas Chamber of Commerce – Paulette, Jeff, and your teams have been awesome supporters and helped us navigate media and communications. We all know our work in this area has only just begun, and we're thankful to be part of such great teams.

To Terri Adams with Schlitterbahn – thank you for the heads up on portable chargers, for always being there when I needed to talk through the next steps, and for being such a friend to Port Royal with your facility here. It's been wonderful to have someone that I could ask all the tough and embarrassing questions too.

And to each of you here with us today, you're a part of our story. And we appreciate you. I'd be happy to stay here all afternoon thanking each of you.

KENDRA

Pat Bell, Director of HR, introduces our Port Royal Strong Foundation and book to the community.

It truly is a privilege to serve along with our Port Royal team. I began my job with Port Royal 6 weeks before the hurricane, and Kendra promised me that this would be the job of a lifetime, but I didn't really understand. Gotta read those offer letters a little closer.

Our employees are truly the heartbeat of what Port Royal Strong represents every single day. While Kendra and the rest of the team have some of the challenges of getting us through, I have the privilege of working with our employees and really just helping them to see, this is where we're going and then getting out of the way because they figure it out on their own.

We had employees who returned to work after the hurricane even after their own homes were damaged. Some were even displaced from their homes. They showed up every day just thankful to have jobs and they wanted to contribute wherever they could, and that's why we're at where we are today. Even though employees were worried about family members and their homes, they came to Port Royal days after the storm when we allowed them to come back, on September 5th. And this is our home also and they wanted to see our home get put back together. And so they were raring to go, so we had to figure out how to corral all that energy and direct them into the right place.

When we realized that working on property was not safe for everyone and was not an option, our employees said, "We're going to Port Aransas. We want to help." We had some employees who lived in Port Aransas we wanted to help, and they wanted to help the community. And we really had to just to organize right after that.

We began doing community service and it really was a therapeutic act for us and our employees. And even though we realized that our home here at PR was not ready to go and it had suffered quite a bit of damage - we realized...our employees realized...that there were a lot of other people who were worse off than we were. We had jobs to come to every day. A lot of people in Port A no longer had jobs, no longer had homes. And we really just extended one of our beliefs, which is Service First...Since we couldn't serve guests here on property, we wanted to serve the community.

The countless hours volunteered to help our community also demonstrated why we wear our Port Royal Strong shirts so proudly. We knew that it meant that Port Royal was taking care of us, and we wanted to do what we could to take care of our community. Whether it was sweeping the streets, gathering the trash, helping people demolish the rest of their property...our team did whatever could be done. And over 17,000 hours of community service had been done just after the hurricane up until we opened again on April 5th. And we're really proud of every one of those hours.

One year later, there are still many employees who have needs from Harvey. Both old needs and new needs. We still have a few employees whose homes are not 100% yet from Harvey. And yet they come to work every day, and they don't have their hand out - they just want to do what they can to put Port Royal back together again. Some of our employees continue to sacrifice even though they're meeting multiple needs of their own family members who may have been displaced and they're taking care of those family members who may not even have jobs still, from Harvey. So we want to do our best to thank our employees. One of the things we realized right after the hurricane is that we didn't have just the employer/employee relationship, but we needed to take care of the whole person. We have decided that we want to continue to help our employees, but we need a vehicle to be able to meet some of those non-traditional employer/employee needs.

So we're proud to announce the Port Royal Strong Foundation that will assist our employees and our community with needs that go beyond that traditional work relationship.

It could be something like mounting medical bills, emergency car repairs, or other unforeseen financial difficulties. We want to return their commitment with our support. We're very excited about not only helping our employees, and we want to continue our commitment and our footprint into the community as well. So our employees will also have a chance to nominate community organizations that are not getting support and it will provide our employees a way to reach out and give in the community.

We like to say that during our recovery we really extended our workplace from right here on property into Port A and into Corpus Christi. We want to continue to exercise our belief, which is Service First as we give to the community. Through the storm, we learned to embrace our larger community, and we invite each of you to join us as we continue to celebrate resilience and getting better.

We aren't celebrating today to just think about the hurricane, but we are celebrating the fact that we've learned this past year, we've gotten stronger, we're a stronger team, and we want to continue to tell that story. We feel like it's a story that we can be very proud of. We want to be a positive example of what can happen when you're recovering from a storm.

As we share our timeline of events, we think that this story will be a story of hope that will help us to all appreciate our journey and the lessons we have learned to continue to demonstrate our resilience of getting better every single day.

I am so, so proud of our employees. And we so appreciate every single thing you have done for us...your prayers, your thoughts, your gifts, and even just your presence. I want you to know that you have changed lives. Many lives.

Whether we had damage to our homes or not, just watching our employees walk through the challenges in their own life and still come here and be so concerned to make sure that Port Royal shines again - thank you so much, because we couldn't do it without you. And that's why we know that we can celebrate - that we are better, we're resilient, and we are absolutely Port Royal Strong.

PAT

Embracing Our New Normal

Things were different, and that was okay.

I think part of building momentum for us was redefining what "normal" is. We've said goodbye to the past in a lot of ways, and we have finally embraced the fact that normal doesn't mean there aren't changes - it's how we operate, regardless of our circumstances. We value interdepartmental collaboration more. One of the most important things we learned as a team overall is that we have to remember we are each other's customers.

We had to live through the pain when we reopened, and understand how we impact each other, have better appreciation for each other's departments and what people have to go through. We've also had to exit employees who did not grasp that new concept - our new definition, new culture. I think that has said a lot - that what we value most is employees bringing 100% and being accountable for their own actions, and working hard to improve the guest experience in spite of our environment.

Throughout the summer we had to improve our communication and redefine expectations. Our conversations had to become very specific and task-oriented. For example, involving multiple departments to walk rooms gave us different perspectives as to what it takes to get one room ready for a family. Team members could then go back to their own departments and share that story with everyone else.

PAT

As far as momentum goes, that's like the perfect description - momentum is very hard to get going at first. It's like trying to get a heavy ball rolling. At first it's really hard, but once you get it rolling, it's a lot easier to keep it rolling than the first initial push. I think that's what we really experienced - it was really hard at first, but our teams kept pushing; we got it rolling, now the machine is oiled and going by itself.

When we opened, and throughout the summer, we were receiving a mixture of feedback from guests; because not everyone knew how significant the damage was. Those that understood what we've been through were happy to support us, and those that expected the best, less than a year after the hurricane, were not so positive. Some guests only experienced minor flooding, not realizing the destruction to our area. When our teams started communicating the realities of our property better, that's when feedback and support improved.

Our ratings for July and August overall are almost just as good as before the hurricane. There is a definite shift in what guests noticed. *Before the hurricane, people would mention the pool, property, and other physical aspects of our resort. Now they mention the guest service and employee attitudes. Almost every review mentions our team members.*

STEPHAN NOACK, DIRECTOR OF REVENUE
& MARKETING

We were AMAZED at the work done at Port Royal since the hurricane. The pool was great and our three bedroom condo was very nice all considered. These people have obviously worked SO HARD to restore Port Royal to the place we love.

They have a ways to go but we can't wait until next summer to see what wonderful updates they have made. Even with work in progress, we had a great time at Port Royal and can't wait to go back. Even a hurricane can't stop the good times from happening at Port Royal! PORT ROYAL, the staff, and Port Aransas in general are Texas at its best!

LINDA & STANLEY D., 07.19.18

We've been going to Port Royal for many years, but this year's trip was probably the best yet. Even though not everything has been restored from the damage of Hurricane Harvey, the work the Port Royal staff has put in over the past year is amazing.

The pools were immaculate, the temporary setups (check-in tent, restaurant and activities) were fine. It also didn't hurt that

*the beaches were the cleanest in recent memory. It was a
great week.*

RANDAL S., 08.10.18

---

*This is our 6th family trip to Port Royal. We were so happy to
see how well it's been restored since the hurricane last year. The
pools were as beautiful as ever and they really improved upon
the guest activities. My kids (10, 13) absolutely loved the
sandcastle building lessons, evening s'mores, karaoke, pool
movie, giant slides, and ninja-warrior style inflatables in all the
pools. Happy kids, happy family.*

DELAYNE V., 09.04.18

We achieved our peak this summer during the Coastal Bend
Veterinarians conference in early September. They join us each
year and were so gracious to return. For their stay, we rented 92%
of the rooms in our four open buildings, and they filled our entire
Event Center and Plaza with activities. The teams even rallied to
show the Aggie Football game in our Cabana Bar on Saturday
afternoon.

It was the perfect closing to an unforgettable summer season.

EPILOGUE

WE WISH this were the end of the story.

The reality is that our journey to recover from Hurricane Harvey will continue for much longer. We have significantly more repairs to complete, and we're still navigating the insurance process.

We debated whether to delay this book until the outcomes were certain, but we also thought it could be helpful to share our experiences along the way. And we decided that it was important for you to know that our lives are already better. We're not waiting for the finish line to choose joy and teamwork.

Plus, if the adventure continues, we can always write a sequel.

If you'd like to keep in touch or support us in this journey, please visit our Foundation website at portroyalstrong.com.

ACKNOWLEDGMENTS

To the team that stayed on property to face the unknown, thank you for your bravery and dedication. None of this would have been possible without that first commitment.

To our Port Royal Board of Directors - Jerry Ellis, Kimberly Kreider Dusek, Bill Mann, Paul Tressa, Scott Farhart, Rich VanBuren, and Buzz Park - who provided constant support and guidance, we appreciate you.

To David Vinson and Rian Glasscock with AmTech Solutions and Signature Group, you stepped up for us from the beginning and have never stepped down – despite many obstacles and challenges. Your commitment and loyalty will never be forgotten.

To our insurance team led by Daniel Carlisle, your preparation and planning are second to none. Your persistence on our behalf goes far beyond anything we could have expected.

To our attorney, Bryan Stone, who has been by our side for years, through every challenge and opportunity, we appreciate your diligence and unparalleled commitment to keep us moving forward.

To State Representative Todd Hunter, and Corpus Christi City Councilmembers Debbie Lindsey-Opel and Greg Smith, we appreciate your support and visits in the immediate aftermath. Your encouragement provided light in a dark time.

To the employees of the City of Corpus Christi, thank you for your flexibility and support. From Development Services to Vector Control and every department in between, we appreciate that you've helped us navigate every obstacle and project.

To Schlitterbahn Corpus Christi, Impact City Church, and our community partners in Port Aransas and Corpus Christi, thank you for opening your doors to our employees when we needed another "home." Your open hearts and welcoming arms were just what we needed to begin healing.

To the Texas State Aquarium who hosted our employees for holiday luncheon and day of fun, thank you for your love and generosity.

To the Port Royal condominium owners who stopped by from week one to offer food, support, and gift cards to assist many employees impacted directly by the hurricane, you provided encouragement that will be remembered forever.

To my friends who visited me while I stayed on property for those first few months, your warm meals and supportive hugs showed me what true friendship looks like. I will always treasure you.

To all of the contractors and vendors who helped rebuild our property, thank you for your contribution. We're learning that it takes an army to recover from a disaster, and we're thankful to have you on our team.

To Brandon Crowson, Kaley O'Brien, and Sarah Perez, the research team who dedicated themselves to reviewing countless documents, videos, interviews, and posts. Your work is the only way we could have made this book a reality. Thank you.

To my Executive Team – Pat Bell, Stephan Noack, Omar Gonzalez, Mellissa Shackelford, and Eric Contreras – your tireless efforts, many unseen works, and relentless commitment ensured we made the best decisions we could at every new turn. We could not have weathered this storm without each of you leading your areas and guiding our teams. I am proud to call each of you my friend and teammate.

To my family who provided much needed support and encouragement during the darkest hours and celebrated the small victories with me, I love you and thank you. (In case you're curious, I still have the Wonder Woman shower shoes.)

Most of all, to the employees of Port Royal who have shown individual fortitude, gratefulness, and unwavering commitment, you each are amazing. You endured the heat, mosquitos, the cold, unrelenting rain, and long work hours, and you did it with pride to prepare our property for guests and owners. Through the countless hours dedicated to assist our community in addition to our property, you showed the heart of service and exemplify "Port Royal Strong." Your spirit is forever etched in the foundation of our property and will never be forgotten. Our Board of Directors, Executive Team, owners, guests, and community recognize that we have something special at Port Royal. We have shown that we are more than brick and mortar. We are a team with a common bond that makes us stronger every day. It is a privilege to be your General Manager, and I appreciate getting to be on your team.

Ruby Acuna • Sales Manager • 3 years

My favorite memory at Port Royal was seeing the first student jump into the pool after the hurricane mess. The buses pulled in, the students got off, took their stuff to their rooms, and came down immediately to the pool. I remember, there was this one kid - he was the first one to jump in, just happy to be there. I was just so happy. I felt like, we are back to normal. That was the best. It brought tears to my eyes!

Patricia Bell • Director of HR • 1 year

My first day was 7 weeks before the hurricane. I truly believe I was in the right place, at the right time for the right reason. It has been the best experience to demonstrate how human resources can be much more the policies and procedures. Building the connection for our employees through this journey and finding powerful meanings through lessons we have all been taught will be with me for a lifetime.

Valerie Borden • Lifeguard/Aquatics • 2 years

I have learned different tasks throughout this rebuilding process. We were able to step up, lead teams, and assist in the clean-up process in Port Aransas.

I am thankful for the opportunity. I am able to say I know every employee here at Port Royal. I am honored to be an employee for Port Royal.

Anita Borden • Housekeeper • 18 years

When we came back we started cleaning rooms, we had to wear a hard hat. The best thing was when we got to ride the big charter bus to community service - I had never been in a bus that big before. They picked us up so we could go do service in Port Aransas. It was nice!

Elaine Brooks • F&B Supervisor • 12 years

While we were working in the community, I realized that there was so much good out there. I was amazed and saw the kindness of my co-workers that worked so hard in Port Aransas, and their assigned community service. I enjoyed working at Metro Ministries and was very proud to represent Port Royal there. I'm very blessed with my employment here at Port

Royal. I have met some wonderful people here. I'm pretty proud to tell people that I work here.

Ted Byrd • AC Technician, Maintenance • 1 year

I really enjoyed helping other people. Just because we went through a crisis did not mean we had to stop doing what we were doing. We had a good momentum going right before the storm. We really wanted to help others; it made us feel good. We did the best we could to help out the most we could. Our standards were a lot higher than most places in the area. It was a great experience.

Hilda Cantu • Housekeeping Manager • 13 years

After the hurricane, we were able to pull through this tragedy, survive, and overcome, and we're still working! We have guests coming! That's great. There are people out there that believe in us, that still want to come out here. I will do my best and so will my team - to make sure these rooms look good. That's what it amounts to - to make those guests happy and make those memories. I'm honored to to be here.

Maria Chavez • Housekeeper • 11 years

I like working for Port Royal because I have a lot of friends here. We volunteered at Salvation Army, the Food Bank, Habitat for Humanity, and in Port Aransas. I remember cleaning an entire house in Port A for a woman that was unable to clean. My favorite memory is when the foreign exchange students would come and help us in housekeeping, it was always a lot of fun.

Eric Contreras • Director of Facilities • 3 Months

I joined the Port Royal team on July 23, 2018. During the hiring process getting to meet some of the staff, I felt very welcomed and I knew this was the right fit for me. I bring to this role over 20 years of Directorship experience in operations, business development, service, human resources, and management. I am a native Texan and have been married to my wife for 27 years. Together we have three children, three grandchildren and two dogs; my passion is my family and my pets.

Ahlea Cormier • Housekeeping Clerk • 2 years

I remember coming back to property seeing nothing but seagrass everywhere. Seeing pictures online did not do justice to the damage that has been done. I had just had my son, Zaydan. I remember taking pictures to show him what we went through

when he was born. I feel our teams are much stronger and, I am fortunate to be part of the Port Royal Strong family.

Brandon Crowson • F&B Supervisor • 1 year

I started working for Port Royal roughly a year and a half ago. I began working as a pool server however, within a few short weeks, Cousin Harvey (as Pat calls it) made landfall. I remember coming back to property two days after the storm, walking rooms, escorting owners and assisting maintenance replacing door locks. After a couple weeks of clean up, I was asked to join the Insurance Team with Omar. I was able to work closely with Mrs. Dusek and leadership here at Port Royal. After we had assisted in all we could do, I was then was tapped to join the Owner Communication Team. Having the opportunity to work closely with our owners was a remarkable experience. I would have never thought the amount of kindness, generosity, and support so many owners showed me. At the time of reopening, I was brought back to the Food and Beverage department to help run operations for our busiest time of the year. It was a challenge operating with drastic differences in provided amenities. Recently, I have had the privilege of being a member on the Special Project Team. Working closely with Sarah, Kaley, Pat, Noack, and Kendra assisting in research and other given tasks has been such a great experience. Many friendships have been made along the way, and the bond between employees has strengthen. I can truly say I enjoy working for such an amazing company such as Port Royal. I can not wait to see how high we bounce back. We are #PortRoyalStrong.

Joe DeAses • Guest Services Supervisor • 3 years

My favorite memory is from last year, we were under the tent and we had a pot luck on my birthday. Brandon was Santa Claus, and after that we had a week off for Christmas. It was pretty cool. We are like a family out here now, after the storm we just have a different kind of respect for each other.

Melissa Dixon • Reservations Manager • 12 years

Coming out of this recovery, our Management Team has learned to work better together. We have a solid team now! One example: it was all hands on deck right after the hurricane trying to get the rooms back together for our groups coming in. All the managers stepped up to get the work done, whether that included cleaning rooms with housekeeping, staging them, scraping texture, etc. Seeing everyone come together like that make you proud to be a part of this team no matter the situation!

Rosa Fielder • Housekeeping Supervisor • 26 years

It is different now from what I started, everything always changes. I remember the Christmas parties have always been fun. Every year goes by so fast that you don't even realize that you have been here that long, and we keep busy. I don't like that Harvey had to change everything, I miss my 2 building. It was my building for a long time, and now I had to change to 3 building. I remembered every single room and what they had and if anything went missing. There was an owner once that was missing one of her dining chairs, and I was able to go in and find it. When the owners came they were so happy, and it made me feel good that I was able to help.

Richard Flenniken • Dishwasher • 17 years

One of my favorite memories was in 2010 when I was the employee of the year. While working here, I have learned not to sweat the small stuff. After the Hurricane, I volunteered with Port Royal at the Salvation Army. I was prepping for the lunch, cleaning after the lunch, and washing the dishes when needed. It made me realize that my plight was not all that bad, there were some people that didn't even have a house.

Brian Friou • Driver/Maintenance • 13 years

Working in Port A with community service, when we found the ashes for the woman whose home was destroyed. She couldn't find her husband's ashes and we found them for her. It made me feel good that we could do that.

Debbie Fuessel • Owner Team Manager • 7 years

One of my favorite memories is the very first time we were able to have an All Hands meeting after Harvey. Several people were affected, it was powerful to see everyone there again. We were all together, here we are and what's going on. My knowledge base is much wider since Harvey, I know a lot more about construction, water intrusion, contractors, scraping mud off floors. I know a lot more than I ever thought I'd know and I know more people than I ever thought I would meet. Like contractors, I would have never met if it were not for this. They are people I could sit down and talk to and feel comfortable with. I'm so glad to have had this privilege.

Delia Gonzalez • Reservations • 3 Years

I feel really comfortable here at Port Royal. I have worked call centers for the past 17 years. Feeling more of a person with a

meaning rather than just a number, is amazing. Loyalty with my employer was the reason I stayed post Harvey. I have learned patience is a virtue when it comes to recovering from a major disaster like Hurricane Harvey. Unlike many other hotels in the area that aren't open yet, we are and it is a great opportunity talking to guest helping them plan their family vacations. The training programs were excellent especially for those employees that have never been through a customer service training. Our reservations team members were also able to spend some time outside of the call center to assist in the volunteer work other employees were doing. Unfortunately, due to my disability I was not able to assist in those opportunities but, I was able to stay here in the call center and talk to guest on a daily basis. Today, talking to new time guests that are understanding on our situation, and simply want to support and help others.

Omar Gonzalez • Director of Operations • 3 years

I started as the Director of Resort Operations, over Food & Beverage and Retail. Now I cover all of Operations and guest-facing areas, including Food & Beverage, Retail, Housekeeping, and Guest Services. My favorite thing about working here is that - unlike other corporate environments where you're just a name or another employee - here you're part of the team, part of the family. You can see the impact of your actions on the team, organization, and guests, if not immediately, then eventually. To see that and be a part of it is very fulfilling.

Curtis Goode • General Helper/Projects • 5 years

I have learned that it benefits a person to help someone. I come to work and do the best job that I can. One of the main things that I try to leave with every guest and owner, I always give my name and tell them that they can ask me anything. It might be big or small, but I'll do my best to help. I hear a need, and I try to follow it out. Port Royal has done so much for me.

Brent Grant • Guest Services Supervisor • 10 years

I won employee of the year twice in a row. It felt great that people recognized all I did. I was a GSA - called a Courtesy Officer at that time. It was to show recognition to the person that went above and beyond and worked the hardest that year. My job was really challenging, and just to be recognized was awesome.

John Grant • Pool Technician • 5 years

When I sit back and think of all the things that have happened these last few months, I can't help but think of the day that we all came back. It is my favorite memory,

only because I was able to see everyone and I knew that our team was all okay. I think that we were a strong team before Harvey, but after we did community service together in Port A and came back to help on property we are all way closer. I know that other teams are working just as hard as we are, and I want to help them in any way that I can.

We just have a better understanding of each other and we know that we can get anything accomplished if we work together. We all have the same goal at the end of the day.

Brian Grant • Lifeguard • 10 years

From doing community service after the hurricane, I've learned that people are happy when you help them in a moment of distress.

Sabrina Grubbs • Aquatics Manager • 5 years

I am currently managing my fourth department since my time here. I really enjoy working for Port Royal, mainly because of the flexibility to learn, grow, and make mistakes along the way. I currently am the aquatics manager, leading a team of over 30 lifeguards during peak season. I decided to stay working with PR for multiple reasons. I really enjoy the fun we have every day. We work hard every day but, you look around and all the employees

have a smile on their face, laughing with each other. Seeing friendly faces such as returning guests is awesome. Port Royal has invested in each and every one of us through training seminars, conventions, etc. I remember specifically the day, April 5, seeing the first school buses arrive on property. That day truly showed the resilience between all of our teams. There were many people that doubted us and our decisions to re-open so soon. However, seeing those kids get off the bus, smiles on their faces, all our leadership team assisting in check-ins and getting kids to their rooms. We did it. We made it happen. It was remarkable moment. We all chose the mentality we had every day. Choose who you want to be on a daily basis. That's what helped us get to where we are today.

Spencer Iezzi • Network Administrator • 3 years

One of my favorite memories was staying late on property for multiple nights to fix the cabling with our on-property team. I felt that I really got to know others outside my department much better than ever before. It was a big job and there were a lot of long nights, but we had people from Food & Beverage, HR, and other departments helping out to get the job done. We really came together as a team during that time.

Martha Knight • Marketing Manager • 4 years

My favorite memory at Port Royal is post Harvey. I distinctly remember working closely with the sales team to bring a great summer experience to life. The best part of this was not coming up with the ideas, but making it happen. It made me feel like I was part of something bigger than my department, especially after seeing all the smiles and great feedback from guests.

Jim Kunau • Senior Guest Services Manager • 4 Months

When I first moved to Corpus Christi, I stayed in a unit for a month. I fell in love with the property. Over the course of the next few years, I began meeting members of the team. I watched them mesh as a team and I was envious . When the opportunity came to join the team, I jumped at the chance. Their devotion to the project and each other was apparent. I am still as excited as the day I said yes. And I believe the commitment of the team has increased since my arrival. I'm pleased to be a part of the team.

Anna Martinez • Housekeeping Supervisor • 1.5 Years
You see the difference since the storm. One day we had everything, and then we didn't have water or electricity. You learn to appreciate everything that you have. While we were

out doing community service, we loved the food bank, they had such a friendly environment. Being able to help people that lost all their belongings by packing food for them was nice.

Felisha Martinez • Server • 5 years

It was great getting to know more of the employees after the storm. A lot of employees before didn't know us because we had three places to come for food, and now everyone is limited on their options because of Harvey. I learned to work with other people, I was always used to working by myself. Working in the restaurant, I had to learn how to work more as a team, and help others. I never had the opportunity to work with them pre-Harvey.

Bonney Maurer • Safety Manager • 9 years

The truth is, there is no major favorite memory that I have, but so many small memories that revolve around being a team. There are all the lifeguards that go on to help people in the community as they go about their day to day life. Many of them have contacted me years after they quit lifeguarding, and moved into their careers, that there was a circumstances that they were able to assist with thanks to their experiences here at Port Royal.

In addition to lifeguards go out and saving lives, it is always touching to see our teams assisting each other, or being excited to help others like we saw after Hurricane Harvey. Vague I know, but truthfully, the best stuff in my book.

Bill McCutcheon • Maintenance • 23 years

I won the first Employee of the Year award...of course it was the first time they did it. I have learned a lot from Port Royal in plumbing, electrician, and AC technician. I even learned to manage a little bit and how to deal with people. This is the only place I've been for 22 years. This is the only job I wanted to have for the rest of my life. They're gonna have to carry me off in an ambulance.

Tressy Merrill • Human Resources • 4 years

My favorite memory was when employees came and cleaned the RV park for me so I could go home. I was living in Flour Bluff, and the RV park I lived at in Port Aransas called me to say they were trying to get me back into my spot, but they needed help cleaning up. Port Royal sent like 70 people over there that day. I remember driving up to the park, and they were all out there cleaning. I was just balling. They cleaned it so I could go home. That was a big thing for me. They all said, "we're doing this for you, Tressy."

Roger Montalvo • Human Resources • 1 year

I like the fact that he hurricane brought us together - the camaraderie working on tasks, duties, etc. The unknown - never knew what you were going to do from day to day. Coming to work, you never knew what you were going to do that day. When you don't know - you don't stress about it. You just dive in, and it just all comes together. It was chaos out here the first few weeks - we were just out here cleaning up all the rubble, coming up with a plan as we went.

Stephan Noack • Director of Revenue & Marketing • 9 years

Since I started in 2009, the changes that I've seen at Port Royal have been quite exceptional. I remember when we started our Port Royal University. Seeing the changes in our teams - not only in their work lives - but also in personal areas, has been amazing. I'm so proud of the journey that we've been on and what we've been able to accomplish over the last year. It's amazing how much community service, training, and building relationships can do for a company's culture.

Kaley O'Brien • Marketing & Events Coordinator • 6 months

When I started working with Port Royal at the beginning of the summer, I was immediately inspired by the resilience and determination of the team here. It was apparent as I drove up to the property for the first time that things were not perfect. What was even more apparent, though, was the heart that each and every person put into serving guests and making up the difference where our property fell short. After working here for just 6 short months, I can say that I've learned more about service and perseverance than ever before. Port Royal Strong is not just a reference to the hurricane anymore, but rather a part of our culture and a way of life for us every day. I hope to contribute to this story, through this book and through the work I do each day, to bring fun and joy to our guests. It is a privilege to be a part of this team.

Kaylynn Paxson • Senior F&B Manager • 4 Months

I started in early August 2018, and have been so honored to be able to count myself a part of such an incredibly resilient team! Being from Corpus Christi, and having experienced the joys and sometimes challenges that come with living and working in a coastal area, joining a team in the recovery phase after Hurricane Harvey was an opportunity for which I was very thankful and excited to offer help from my own personal experiences and background. It's been a true joy to be a part of the journey where we are focusing on rebuilding and strengthening strategies that will shape the future of this local iconic property. The most rewarding part is feeling and experiencing the strength and unity of the teams that make the execution of this project possible, everyday. Coming to work and looking forward to working with these great people make everyday something to feel excited about and continue to look to the future! #PortRoyalStrong

Sarah Perez • Human Resources • 2 years

I started at Port Royal two years ago part time, and I never could have imagined that we'd be where we are today. After Harvey I was given so many opportunities to learn and grow, not only in my position, but as a person as well. Some days are harder than others, but I am constantly inspired by those around me. When I first started I'd say we were a strong team, but now we are #PortRoyalStrong! It doesn't matter what gets thrown our way, we are a resilient team. Our comeback is always bigger than our setback. I can't wait to see what the future has in store for this team!

John Reyes • Controller • 4 years

My favorite thing about being at Port Royal is being able to work with such great people. This has been the most difficult time to be here, but in the midst of all the chaos the employees stayed unified to achieve each other's

goals. We understand there are still obstacles ahead but as long as we stick together, we can overcome anything.

Maria Reynolds • Housekeeping

After Harvey, I was sick - I'm just really happy that Port Royal kept me and I got to keep working once I was able to come back. I went to volunteer at Dress for Success and the Salvation Army. We put all the stuff away, priced the clothes, vacuumed, swept, clean the restrooms every day. We helped give the toys away to the kids at Salvation Army. We also worked for Habitat for Humanity and the Food Bank. We got to make boxes with the First Lady when she came to visit. We had fun going to all those different places, it would be nice to have a chance to do something good for the community like that again.

Vicara Rivers • Server • 17 years

It's been 17 years of happiness. I'm proud to be a part of Port Royal. People care for each other. I lived in Port Aransas before Hurricane Harvey. Our community lost so much - many didn't have a job or a place to live. My house took a lot of damage, too. But Port Royal allowed me to take off for a month to clean up and get everything together, and they still paid

me during that time. That was so cool. It was necessary, and I am so grateful.

Leocadia Ruiz • Housekeeper • 13 years

Cleaning the church, mopping and talking to people you already know. In the food bank, we liked to put food in the boxes. The wife of the president came to see us. We helped sort food for the NPW Community Outreach on the Island. At the Dress for Success, we organized everything - all the clothes by type and color.

Vivien Sanchez • Former F&B Manager • Moved to Seattle

I am so grateful for the time I was able to spend at Port Royal. While we were out doing community service in Port A, it really gave us a different perspective. I'm glad that I had the opportunity to work at Port Royal and gain experience from my job and from helping the community.

Mellissa Shackleford • Director of Finance • 3 years

I felt that I could call Port Royal my second home and have since the day I started. One of the most compelling things I have learned since the hurricane is the we are all much stronger than what we realize when we trust our own judgement and work as a team. There are days there was so much to figure out. It can be overwhelming, from the high-level financial and insurance aspect, to getting the halls swept and toilets cleaned. As we work though these long days, we have each other to lean on. It might be needing someone to to remind you to focus on one thing at at time, reminding you how far we have already come, to remind you to take a break or just support on a personal level for each other. We have many staff that were affected tremendously by the storm. The compassion shown to us was exceptional at every level. We still have a ways to go but it astonishing to me that we have come this far by our faith in one another. This world is your best teacher. There is a lesson in everything. There is a lesson in each experience. Learn from it and become wise. Every failure is a stepping stone to success. Every difficulty or disappointment is a trial of your faith and determination. Every unpleasant incident is a test of your inner strength. You just keep working together, marching forward and do the next best thing.

Donald Smith • Maintenance • 19 years

For the past nineteen years, I have been privileged to work in the Facilities and Maintenance department here at Port Royal. Port Royal has always been good to their employees. We have always had the family "vibe" here between

us all. There's quite a few people that have been here for a long time, like myself. We all work well with each other. I remember my favorite memory is after Hurricane Harvey. The community service and volunteer opportunity was inspiring. We had the ability to bond with others we weren't able to work with at all before the storm. It has been a rough ride. You must stay focused. There are many hills but, you have to have the end in mind. It has worked for me.

Mel Spencer • F&B Manager • 3 years

My hurricane experience was probably more extreme than some other employees because the entire restaurant was destroyed. My staff and I had to learn how to do our jobs adapting to new environments. We are currently working out of our third mobile trailer since October 2017. Our event center functions as a dining room for food service, banquets, meetings, and Sunday brunch. Creating a workable menu for each location and event, executing the food and service, and finding storage space for everything we need to make events happen has been very challenging to overcome. We have not failed an event so far and continue to fight to prevent that from happening.

John St. Clair • Food & Beverage • 17 years

I was hired as a dishwasher, I applied here because I was referred by a job coach. I do prep work and dishwashing. My favorite part about my job is the people, I get along with everybody. Since the hurricane I have learned that you can't predict the weather.

Crysta Stuart • Guest Services • 2 years

The Christmas party out on property after the storm. It was informal, just the people on property. We had a palm tree Christmas tree, and brought gifts for the gift drawing. It was a potluck, and Brandon dressed as Santa. The whole department is almost full of new people, we have a new team and we get along great.

William Tave • Maintenance • 1 year

It's been an experience, but I'm still here. I didn't die. I didn't quit. I've learned to step back, take in the situation, realize that there's nothing I can do about some things, then do my best to fix the problem. The biggest thing about going through the hurricane was just not knowing. I have learned to adapt. You've got to do a little bit of everything. I like that. I like working for maintenance, getting calls, talking to people, and fixing things. I love making people happy out here.

Chad Tiffany • Projects • 1 year

Teamwork is my favorite thing, everyone out there through Port A and everyone worked together. I have become a better person, I learned a lot about myself and others through this experience.

Renee Tilley • Housekeeping Supervisor • 6 years

It is always the satisfied guests that make me happy, because that lets me know that the effort and teamwork was successful. I have definitely matured since Harvey. I am emotionally, and spiritually stronger because I was a huge baby when I first got here. Socially I am more comfortable with other employees not just in my team, but with the other departments too.

Ernie Tipton • Projects Manager • 2 years

Creating the Managers' Boot Camp is my favorite memory. The ability to put all the managers together to create a stronger management team for Port Royal - I have become a better manager, I have new experiences and

found new ways to navigate through difficult situations. From working so closely I am now confident that I have an entire team to back me up if I need help.

Erin Todd • Sales Manager • 2 years

I've learned to have attainable goals in order to adapt to our new working conditions. It was also great being part of the unofficial "spirit team" in the summer. We hosted activities at Port Royal and supported our community on July 4th by passing out fans, glow sticks, and bringing the Port Royal "spirit." We brought a lot of joy not only to our guests and to the Port Aransas community, but to other team members as well.

Matt Trent • F&B Manager • 4 Years

When summer first gets going and the first week of peak season, it's my favorite. It's exciting. It's like the build up is over and now it is time to execute and make guests happy. Port Royal has given me the opportunity to be a manager and develop my leadership capabilities. I think just being on the beach makes this job more fun. It's a great view. We work everyday where people pay to take a vacation.

Luis Villarreal • Guest Services • 2 years

There's so many memories. Coming back from the storm - seeing how everybody had come together. Because all of us needed it at that time. It's my other family. We sometimes fight like brothers and sisters, but we love each other. It's kind of a carefree atmosphere here - we are a resort, and our work is serious, but we also have fun.

Tye West • Guest Services Manager • 8 years

Over the 8 years that I've been here, I have become a more confident, resilient, and adaptable person. As the Front Office Manager, I've face many situations and scenarios that required me to step outside of my comfort zone. Prior to hurricane Harvey, we expected to take on our days with a percentage of uncertainty. Post Harvey, we had to remind ourselves and each other to remain adaptable. Understanding our new journey will be full of change and the greater percentage of uncertainty, was most important. Although many days were hectic and very challenging, they were character building. I would not be the confident, resilient, adaptable person I am today had I not gone through our "new normal."

I welcome and look forward to the new chapter and continued journey with Port Royal Resort.

Dalton Womble • Guest Services • 4 months

Working here, I've learned to take a breath. No matter how busy and hectic it gets out here, you have to learn to take a breath, otherwise you'll get upset. And there's no point. My whole job is to make our guests happy, and if I'm not happy, I won't be able to do that.

John Yarbrough • Projects • 21 years

It was the only job that was in town, so I came to work here. After the hurricane I was working out in Port A, it is my town. Before Port Royal, I worked primarily to clean my neighborhood; there were not many places that wanted help. I was one of the first people that they brought back to property, I was excited to be back. We had a lot of work to get done and we still do. You don't know where to start; there are so many things that need to be fixed. Things look so much better now, after Harvey this place was a disaster area.

Bryan Young • Former Aquatics Supervisor • 3 years

I started in June of 2015 as a Lifeguard and told Bonney I would like to be more than a lifeguard; However, Bonney said I had to fit with the team and work up. I put all the time I could to do whatever I could to help. Port Royal poured into me, sent me to so many trainings and I was able to step into a teaching role as the Lifeguard Supervisor. This helped me mentally; it was a lot more with first aid, customer interactions, and guest issues. It helped give me a service attitude and gave me the ability to improve the guest experience. I want to thank Port Royal for the opportunity and the culture that you created. It is an outstanding company; you go above and beyond. It is inspiring to know that there are companies out there with the mindset to take care of their employees even when they don't have to. Keeping us and training us was a great thing to do. I pray that people can take out of this that you can be dedicated to your community and employees and come through on top. Doing so much for us made us want to do so much for Port Royal in return.

Sarah Zieglar • Reservations Supervisor • 11 years

I take pride in working at a property that cares for the community and also has the best accommodations. I like that we are now recognized as more than just a hotel in the community - people have seen our impact since the hurricane. We really are the best - no one else has what we have. I'm proud to work here.

Our Executive Team: Kendra Kinnison, Omar Gonzalez, Stephan Noack, Mellissa Shackelford, Pat Bell, and Eric Contreras

Kendra L. Kinnison, MBA, CPA, is the General Manager for Port Royal Ocean Resort. Kendra serves on the Board of Directors for the Texas Travel Industry Association, the Board of Directors for the Corpus Christi Convention and Visitors Bureau, the Board of NavyArmy Community Credit Union, and the Advisory Board of the College of Business at Texas A&M University - Corpus Christi. She chairs the Texas BPW Foundation and is a Past State President of Texas Business Women. Over the last two decades, Kendra has served in leadership positions in a number of community service organizations.

Holding an MBA and BBA from Texas A&M University - Corpus Christi, Kendra is the youngest MBA graduate in the school's history. She is also a graduate of Leadership Corpus Christi Class XXX and was the Steering Committee Chair for Class XXXV. Kendra was an inaugural selection to Corpus Christi's Top 40 Under 40 list in 2006 and was a Y Women in Careers Honoree in 2005.

twitter.com/kkinnison

instagram.com/kkinnison

READY TO BE A PART OF OUR STORY?

VISIT US AT
PORTROYALSTRONG.COM

Made in the USA
Lexington, KY
30 November 2018